SEVEN PLUS

SEVEN PLUS

by Margaret V. Old

SCRIPTURE UNION
5, Wigmore Street, London, W1H 0AD

© Scripture Union 1972
First published 1972

ISBN 0 85421 340 6

Printed by A. McLay & Co. Ltd., Cardiff and London

CONTENTS

Introduction. What's Your Score?   9

1. Getting to know . . . whom?   13

2. Seven to eleven   23

3. Look out! Children!   32

4. What are we trying to do?   42

5. Now I'm a teacher . . .   51

6. Children, God and the Bible   63

7. Let's be flexible   73

8. Learning through doing   82

9. Making it live   92

10. Using their eyes   99

11. Hands together and eyes closed?   110

12. What about music?   116

Introduction

WHAT'S YOUR SCORE?

Knowing yourself is very important. Whatever your work among boys and girls, put yourself in each of these situations and give what you think would be your honest answers.

Your situation	Your reaction
1. You have a group of children in your home each Sunday. You know that birthdays mean a lot to children, and you have the date of birth of every child in your group.	*Do you* (a) notice the dates, and mention each birthday the Sunday after it occurs, asking the child to tell you about it? (b) send every child a birthday card, and mention his birthday the following Sunday? (c) remember some birthdays and forget others—or ignore them all?
2. You know that it's a good thing to include activity in your teaching, giving the children plenty to do.	*Do you* (a) decide that it really isn't possible on your premises? (b) decide that some of your difficulties *can* be overcome, and plan so that children *are* able to more than just sit? (c) let the children draw pictures at the end of every lesson as this needs little space and equipment and no preparation?

Your situation	Your reaction
3. You have just been asked to help with a children's meeting and your first assignment is to lead in prayer.	*Do you* (a) make no preparation and at the time pray from an adult's viewpoint *about* the children? (b) try to find out about the children's experience and interests, and pray on their behalf in their language? (c) get the children to say the Lord's Prayer and then follow it with another prayer you learned at school?
4. You are a Sunday School teacher in the middle of a very busy week, and have yet to prepare next Sunday's lesson.	*Do you* (a) do it now, missing your favourite television or radio programme? (b) do it late on Saturday night? (c) leave it till some time Sunday morning?
5. The worst 'little horror' is absent. What is your first reaction?	*Do you* (a) breathe a silent sigh of relief? (b) feel sorry he'll miss some teaching which might have done him a world of good? (c) decide when you can go round to his home and find out if he is ill?

Your situation	Your reaction
6. You help with a children's club and keep on intending to visit the homes of the children, but it seems difficult to find time.	*Do you* (a) go on hoping, thinking you're bound to have more time later in the year? (b) admit that you're very reluctant to do visiting, and decide you really must go— soon? (c) pray about your reluctance, and fix a definite date and time when you are going to begin?
7. You sometimes have to give a children's talk in a service. This usually includes telling part of a Bible story in your own words.	*Do you* (a) imagine you are there as you describe both sights and sounds and feelings of people in the story? (b) stick strictly to what is given in the Bible, adding nothing more? (c) let your imagination conjure up incidents as well as sights, sounds and feelings?

Score points as follows:

1	(a) 2	2	(a) 1	3	(a) 1	4	(a) 3
	(b) 3		(b) 3		(b) 3		(b) 2
	(c) 1		(c) 2		(c) 2		(c) 1
5	(a) 1	6	(a) 1	7	(a) 3	Add up
	(b) 2		(b) 2		(b) 2	your total
	(c) 3		(c) 3		(c) 1	score.

What was your score?

7 *points*   Don't despair! Christian work among children is not easy—though very worthwhile—and problems, shared with God, can vanish. Read this book, put it into action—and try the quiz again. You may score 21!

8–14 *points*   What if you do still have a lot to learn? At least you know it and can start learning. Don't forget, however, that head knowledge is not enough; it must be put into practice.

15–20 *points*   Well done! But don't rest on your laurels; there may not have been a question on your weak spot! As you read this book, list anything that you think *you* specially need to remember, and act upon it.

21 *points*   You may well feel pleased with yourself—but don't sit back too contentedly. There's always something more to learn about understanding and teaching children. No two children are alike. And if you are mastering the art of teaching, could you lead a training group, using this book as a basic text-book? See p. 124.

Whatever your score was

If you are endeavouring to bring boys and girls to an understanding of the Christian faith, remember that understanding is not enough. They need to come to a living experience of Jesus Christ—to meet Him and to own Him, Friend, Saviour and Lord. With an aim like this before you, you need to know Him in the same way yourself, and to be equipped to meet the attacks that Satan will make on your work among the children. Never forget that you are not alone in a task to which God has called you. 'We are ambassadors for Christ, God making His appeal through us,' those who are 'working together with him' (2 Cor. 5. 20; 6. 1).

Chapter One

GETTING TO KNOW - WHOM?

Children are not learning machines. They are people in their own right, who need to be understood as *children*—**not as mini-adults— and someone or something must cause them to** *want* **to learn.**

Martin is a new boy. He has come because his friend does. At the moment he is not at all interested in what it means to be a Christian. Anyway, he assumes it is nothing but trying to be good all the time—and that does not appeal to him in the least! If he is to learn from Miss Jones, she must first create the right relationship between herself and Martin. The first thing he will be trying to find out is not, 'What is she trying to teach me?' but 'What is she like?'

Think back to your own school-days. What was your most-disliked subject? Can you think of someone with whom you did not get on well, someone who also taught you that subject? It is very likely that you can. Your relationship with that teacher affected both your interest in the subject and your ability to learn.

13

Effective learning—learning that sticks and is acted upon—depends largely on interest and wanting to learn. That in turn depends very much on the relationship set up between learner and teacher. The teacher is anybody who is trying to gain the interest and attention of someone else and to pass on what he knows.

Relationships then are of vital importance—but how does one *build* the right relationship? A relationship with a group is basically a relationship with every individual in that group—so let's start there.

GETTING TO KNOW INDIVIDUAL CHILDREN

What ways are there of getting to know each individual child? Look at each picture and write down what you think *you* could do to get to know children better.

Now read on.

A. Observation

Can you watch children at play—without being too obtrusive—to see how children talk to and behave towards one another? Why not watch one child particularly and see how he or she reacts to different boys or girls?

B. Listening

This is very important. Today's children sometimes lack someone at home who will *really* listen. Learn to be a good listener—and arrange things so that you arrive at Sunday School, club, or whatever it may be *before* the children. Then there will be time to listen as you won't be rushing around with last-minute preparations.

C. and E. Finding out

Do you know what the children like to watch, read and do? Why not ask them? Be careful, however, not to look horrified or to sound too critical—even if you do not really approve of everything they tell you. If their parents do not censor their reading or viewing, should you try to do so—and perhaps set up antagonism in the home?

D. and F. Sharing their interests

Do you ever *do* things together with the children? You will have to *make* time and opportunity for this, and a week-night club can be most valuable. If this supplements teaching given on a Sunday, it should not be planned as a 'meeting' but as a club. Activities can include games, model-making, hobbies, crafts, and a 'Do-it-together' Bible reading time when children read a Bible passage, answer a question about it, ask any questions they may have, and work out what can be prayed about. Such clubs must have a fairly small age-range if they are to be enjoyed and of any lasting value; 7's to 11's or 9's to 13's can be grouped together, but 5's to 15's or even 5's to 11's, will prove more than difficult. More details about the organization of a week-night club for Juniors will be found in *Today's Children, Tomorrow's Church* (Scripture Union).

Now do this test

If you are already teaching or leading a group of children, test how well you really know them.

● Which child in the group had a birthday most recently?

(1 *point if you know.*)

● Did you send a birthday card?

(1 *point if you did.*)

● Can you name three things of interest to those in your group, one of which came into your conversation or teaching last week?

(3 *points if you can: 2 if you can only think of two or if you can name three but did not mention one of them last week: 1 if you can think of only one.*)

● Have you visited the home of every child in the group during the last six months?

(2 *points—1 if you have visited some.*)

● Do you know why every child absent from your group last week was away?

1 *point if you do—and we'll give you this point if there was* 100% *attendance!*)

● Does every child in the group know where *you* live?

(1 *point if the answer is 'Yes' and an additional point if they have all been inside your home at some time—not necessarily all at once!*)

That gives a possible ten points—so how well *do* you know the children in your group? From this test, can you make a list of things to do to show your interest in and concern for each child?

THOSE WHO KNOW THE CHILDREN BEST

No one on earth knows us quite as well as those with whom we live. Just think how well you could get to know Johnnie if you were to *live* with him for a week!

That may be possible—if the leaders of your group are able to organize a residential holiday week for the children. Alternatively, a week-end may be possible. (Practical suggestions for organizing something of this kind can be found in *Today's Children, Tomorrow's Church*.)

Even if this is not possible, you can still try to see the children as their own parents see them. Remember this, however—although most parents (especially mothers) find their child an absorbing topic of conversation, they are likely to 'whitewash' their child's true character to an outsider, unless that person is a real and trusted friend of the family.

GETTING TO KNOW THE FAMILY

'Somehow there's never time for visiting,' sighed Sandra.

His Diabolical Highness sat back in smug satisfaction. 'They never recognize *me* behind that problem,' he said.

Satan was wrong, of course; some of us do know what he is up to—but do we sometimes let him get away with it all the same? The only way to make sure visiting is not neglected is to set aside time for it. If you keep a diary—the sort that lists future engagements rather than a private record of the day's high-spots—decide in advance when you will go visiting, and write it down. The next thing to do is to *look* at that diary—and tell Satan where to go when he starts making his suggestions!

'You didn't realize you'd be so busy this week when you planned to go visiting on Tuesday, did you?' he says. 'There's nothing else you *can* postpone . . . and next week might be much better anyway. People won't be indoors in such lovely weather.' His attack may be on a different line, of course.

'Get that nasty feeling in the pit of your stomach about it . . . it's something to be afraid of . . . you won't know what to say . . . they won't want to see you . . . they may shut the door in your face . . . you'll feel humiliated . . .'

He is a liar! He has been from the beginning. The Lord Jesus Christ told us that Satan 'is a liar and the father of lies' (John 8. 44). There is no need to fear any task to which God calls us, since He will give us all we need for the job, will go before us and prepare the way, and will go with us and prompt us. If we *do* feel afraid, or humiliated by something, let us confess our fear, or our pride that has been injured, and ask for forgiveness and new strength. Then let's get on with the job!

If we show a genuine interest in the *whole* child, not just in his spiritual development, most parents will be welcoming. The following practical tips will help:

1. If possible, visit in pairs.
2. Pray before you go and as you approach the front door.
3. Smile when the door opens. Introduce yourself if it is the first visit.
4. Have a reason for going that will be acceptable *to the parents*.
5. Find out if it is an inconvenient time and if the parent would prefer you to come back later.
6. Be friendly and interested. Remember that a non-churchgoing parent may feel very ill-at-ease with you and on the defensive, afraid of being 'got at'.
7. Be prepared to talk about any topic of mutual interest in order to build up a friendly relationship. Be a good listener—and do not try to force the conversation on to a 'spiritual level'.
8. Avoid talking about a child in front of him, except in giving praise.
9. Most children will be glad to see you coming to their homes; show that you are glad to see them. Show an interest in anything in the room that belongs to or has been done by the child. In other words, build up your relationship with the child while you are with him in his own home, and do not neglect him because of your concern to get to know his parents. Be friendly to younger brothers and sisters, too; you may well be teaching them in later years.
10. Do not overstay your welcome.

You may find that some children do not quite know how to react when you visit their homes. This is because you represent one world and home is another. The two need to be brought together (especially for a child in a non-Christian home)—otherwise Christianity may be seen as something for Sundays only. In fact, all the more reason for regular visiting. If a child is unsure of what to do in a new situation—such as having you in his own home, talking to his mother—he may well 'show off' for a while. Help him to feel at ease by showing an interest in something of his own that belongs to the world of 'home'.

'How's that stamp collection going, John? I'd love to see it if you'd show it to me,' will help to bridge the gap that the child senses between his home life and all that you represent.

If you discover anything about the home or family which would be of interest to others in the church, pass it on—but be careful not to betray confidences.

You will find it helpful to keep a notebook, with a page for each child, where you make a note of all you find out about him. This notebook should never be taken to any place where you meet the children—in case you drop it! Use it to help you to pray for each child.

If you are visiting and want to make a written note of anything before you reach home, do not do it where you might be observed.

GETTING TO KNOW WHAT INFLUENCES CHILDREN

There are four big areas of influence upon a child as he grows up— home, school, the neighbourhood, and society in general. If we are to understand the children, we need to think about the total impact of growing up in today's world.

Home

The influence of home and family is immeasurable. Think of one child you know well. What are relationships like between the various people in the home? What is his position in the family—the youngest, who hates to feel 'too small' and struggles to keep up with the others; the eldest, who often bears a great weight of responsibility and is told 'You're old enough to know better'; the middle child, who is so frequently the odd one out; or an only child, who is over-influenced by adult company and lacks the lessons in 'give and take' which other children would provide?

What about the actual house or flat in which a child lives? Is it overcrowded, a place where nothing is private or safe from younger children and there is no room to play? Is it a home where no reading matter exists apart from newspapers and periodicals? Is it a place where no material comfort is lacking? What are the attitudes to other people and to life which a child will 'pick up' there? What kind of moral standards are accepted? Is he over-controlled by adults—or left too much to his own devices?

Neighbourhood

Much the same questions might be asked about the neighbourhood around the child's home. What are the children like with whom he mixes? What are the most widespread attitudes to the church, to authority, to any minority group, to moral behaviour? What kind of sights and sounds meet him daily?

School

If you are ever invited to visit—perhaps on an Open Day—the school to which the children go, this is an opportunity not to be missed. If you were able to be a child again, but at that school, it would most likely be a very different experience from the one *you* had as a child. You would find the emphasis now to be on learning rather than on teaching, on finding out rather than on being told. The children might well be sitting in groups with the teacher moving among them. Instead of having one set text-book, boys and girls might be using work-cards or finding reference books from a small library. Their own work might be produced as home-made 'books' or on wall-charts rather than in exercise books.

In fact, you might not find subjects set out for separate times throughout the day—apart from times for subjects like Music and Physical Education. The children may be working an 'integrated day'—each child moving on from one activity to another at his own rate, and following a topic of interest without trying to label it 'English' or 'Nature Study' or anything else. A child working on a project on rabbits, for example, may do quite a lot of mathematical calculation in working out how much it would cost to feed a rabbit, he may write and illustrate a book about a pet rabbit, discover the places of origin and different characteristics of the various breeds, and so on. He will move from one thing to another and will not think, 'Now it's time for history so I must find out when rabbits were first taken to Australia and what the result has been.'

Some such schools may even have an open-plan building with 'base areas' for various kinds of activity (a painting and craft area, a library and quiet area, a mathematics area, etc.) rather than separate classrooms. Children will be free to move from one teacher to another as they change the nature of the work they are doing.

This means team teaching rather than the more structured approach of a class each with its own room and its own teaching.

All this means that boys and girls are used to finding out for themselves, questioning what they are told, working in a less highly structured system. Knowing this will help us to understand the way they behave under our own leadership and teaching.

Society

Other influences are brought to bear on all of us—children included—largely through the mass media (television, radio, newspapers and magazines, films, posters, etc.). Consider, for example:

● the spread of permissive attitudes—the idea that nothing is absolutely and always wrong in itself but that 'it all depends . . .'—and changed attitudes to authority and the way that it can be influenced;

● the impact of advertising, which sets out to create 'needs' and which may manipulate human instincts and reactions, arouse dissatisfaction and present materialistic 'answers' to problems;

● the scope of technology and the idea that man has outgrown the need of God as he has discovered more and more how scientific research and achievement can improve his world;

● the cult of meaninglessness which underlines much of our pop culture, so that, without realizing it, young people absorb the ideas that life has no ultimate purpose, that escape from it into fantasy or despair is valid, and that one must search for an experience which will transform life in drugs or in eastern religions or in the occult. We need so to pray and teach that boys and girls may *find* that transformation—in Christ. 'If anyone is in Christ, he is a new creation' (1 Cor. 5. 17).

Chapter Two

SEVEN TO ELEVEN

What are They Like?

It is obvious that children live in the house on the corner. A home-made bow and arrow and a skipping rope lie by the front door, and the lawn has that 'knocked-about-by-boy-playing-football' look. Indoors there are comics and books lying on a chair, a half-assembled model aircraft kit on the sideboard, a doll's house in a corner—and loud voices arguing about the ownership of some foreign stamps. David and Sarah are home!

Let's see what all this has to say to the person teaching them on Sunday.

Active and energetic (football, skipping-rope)

Boys and girls in their 'Junior' years are full of life—active and energetic. Most won't want to walk when they could run, or sit still when there is something to kick, slide around or fidget with.

If you are having to teach these children, what would you do? What questions would you ask yourself?

Since children are so active and energetic and at the peak of their muscular development, they *cannot* sit still and listen while an adult talks to them for twenty minutes. *They need opportunity to move, to change from one kind of activity to another, to take an active part in what is happening.* We need not worry unduly if a child *does* fidget; a question addressed directly to him will tell us whether he is really interested and involved or not. The child sitting unnaturally still should cause us more concern. He may be in an emotional turmoil because all is not well between his parents—or he may be developing measles!

Physically skilful

During the middle years of childhood, boys and girls master the arts of throwing and catching, of climbing, skipping and balancing. David is capable of catching Sarah and tying her very securely and swiftly to the lamp-post with that skipping rope, and Sarah won't be incapable of a well-aimed blow. She may not be able to throw as far or as accurately as her brother—but watch what she can do with two balls at once or with that skipping rope. Notice how skilfully David shifts his weight as he climbs a tree and how steady Sarah is on one foot as she plays hop-scotch.

Enthusiastic over a short-lived 'craze'

Each game has its proper season, of course, and while it's all the rage, it will be given almost all a child's spare time and a tremendous amount of enthusiasm. Try to be aware of the current 'craze', and if you can show an interest or contribute to it, do so. Think first, however, before you distribute conkers at the beginning of Sunday School!

Adventure-loving (bow and arrow, adventure stories)

Closely coupled with a child's bounding energy and delight in his own developing skills is his love of adventure. The books he borrows from the children's library reflect this—and so do the comics he so enjoys. *We need to show in our lives, and in what we say about our own experience, that daily life shared with the Lord Jesus Christ is a great adventure.*

Eager to learn—curious

Those comics and books show us yet more about David and Sarah. Their questioning minds have moved on from the 'Why?' of their early childhood to 'Is it true? How did it happen? How does it work?' The comic-style educational magazines show how to look after a hamster, how to conduct a scientific experiment with magnets and 'How explorers reached and discovered North America'.

Juniors tend to think that 'stories' means something untrue. Bible stories can sound so remote from the world they know that they are thought untrue or irrelevant. *We need to draw out the spiritual truth which is our reason for using the Bible story—to show throughout the teaching, not just at the end, how it applies to a child's life today, and to make it quite clear that what we are teaching is true.*

Realistic

The Junior child's realistic, down-to-earth approach is shown, too, in his expectation that language means exactly what it says. 'Pull up you socks' means 'Pull up your socks'—not 'work harder'! Similarly, 'Ask Jesus into your heart' is likely to convey to today's child a mental picture of the literal, physical heart that pumps the blood around the body—a heart which can be replaced with a transplant if need be. It is not unknown for a child to ask 'If a Christian has to have a heart transplant, does he have to ask the Lord Jesus in all over again?' We should not use phrases like this that will cause misunderstanding. Hymns and choruses need to be chosen carefully for the same reason, and if a hymn contains only one 'dubious phrase', that expression should be explained *before* the hymn is sung.

Literalistic, 'concrete' thinkers

Children's comics and annuals often contain puzzles of various kinds. This is the age for 'How many mistakes can you find in this picture?' and 'Can you find five faces hidden in this drawing?' Minds are active as well as bodies, and the younger Junior especially is eager to learn. His mind is beginning to delight in jokes and riddles, to enjoy working out codes and puzzles. Gradually, he will develop the ability to reason, to put facts alongside one another and to reach conclusions from them—but this is a slow process. He is not ready to think in abstract terms.

"with His Angel train before Him"

Eight-year-old Sarah finds it impossible to think about 'justice' or 'unselfishness', 'salvation' or 'sin'. She finds it difficult to see anything except from her own point of view; she is still the centre of her own world. David has developed the ability to think logically about concrete objects, but he is still unable to reason at an abstract level.

A word does not have to be long to be misunderstood, especially when it has more than one meaning. 'The Son of man came to seek and to save' sounds a simple verse, but 'seek' is not a word used by children, and 'save' may convey the idea of keeping for future use—in the way the child's mother is saving trading stamps.

Imaginative and 'hero-worshipping'
Children's play is imaginative. They identify themselves with people in the adult world—and we can make use of this by letting them act

26

some of the Bible stories we use. In her playing with a doll's house Sarah may imagine herself running a home. David may live out the western he saw on television the previous evening.

Games often show who the children's heroes are. David slams his football against the wall—and scores for England, seeing his current football hero in his mind's eye. Sarah is not so likely to identify *herself* with her hero—but she may well, in her later Junior years, have his photo pinned up in the bedroom. She may collect newspaper cuttings about him—as David will collect programmes from the matches he goes to see with his father on Saturday afternoons. This is because they are—

Collectors
Juniors love to collect things—but few will collect any one thing for very long. Enthusiasms are short-lived. If we are running a week-night club for children, we may find it valuable to have an occasional 'hobbies evening' when the children bring along any collections they have and tell the others about these.

Creative
Most will also enjoy making things—from doll's clothes to space stations made from 'junk'. In teaching children, we can make use of this creative instinct by providing opportunities for them to learn through making models, friezes and books (see p. 73).

Their sense of right and wrong
Sarah still sees her mother as the dominating individual in her life, and the things that seem most wrong to her are 'being naughty' or 'disobeying Mummy' or 'answering back'. When Sarah is about nine, her teacher at school will come to the fore, and the influence of school may well be greater than that of the home. Even then, things will be thought of as right or wrong merely because some adult says so.

Sarah sees behaviour in terms of 'black' or 'white'—there is no 'grey'. People are 'goodies' or 'baddies'. David, however, has some general views on right and wrong, which are not simply a matter of behaviour that adults find unacceptable. 'Stealing' and 'murder' begin now to take the place of 'not wiping my feet when I come in'. An eleven-year-old friend of David, who is very intelligent and beginning to show early signs of teenage behaviour, also shows a sense of responsibility to other people and regards as wrong 'not trying to help others'. Right and wrong is not so clear-cut to him, however. He begins to wonder if a lie is *always* wrong, or if it is right to lie so as to spare someone's feelings.

All this must make us think very hard about what we are to say about sin. The young child will tend to think of it as behaviour that is unacceptable to adults—childish naughtiness, which they will grow out of. *We need to show that it is not so much the wrong things we do as the wrong people we are that is so important.* If the greatest commandment is 'Thou shalt love the Lord thy God with all thy heart . . .' (Mark 12. 30), as Christ said it is, then the greatest sin must surely be the failure to keep that commandment.

But no two children are alike!
David and Sarah are different simply because they *are* separate individuals, and no two people are *exactly* alike. David and Sarah are also different because David is eleven while Sarah is only just eight. (It is important to remember here that there can be a bigger difference in mental ability between two children of the same age than between another two with several years' difference in their ages.) David and Sarah are different again because they are interested in different things—because David is a boy and Sarah is a girl.

'Slugs and snails' or 'sugar and spice'?
How sad that the nursery rhyme should have equated boys with 'slugs and snails and puppy-dogs' tails' while girls were described as 'sugar and spice and all things nice'! There are girls who are 'little horrors' as well as boys.

Sarah is only just eight. She is not interested in team games and plays quite happily with either girls or boys of her own age who live in the same area. David, however, has been introduced to football as a competitive game. He and his friends are no longer satisfied merely to kick a ball about; they prefer to have teams and compete against one another. They want to play with boys only and the 'gangs' or 'clubs' that are formed from about the age of nine are usually single-sex groups.

In some Sunday Schools, boys and girls are kept in separate classes—largely because this is the way things have been done in that church for many years. In fact, the custom probably dates back to the time when the boys and girls were in separate classes in their day schools, even at the age of seven or eight. For most children, this is no longer the case. Let's look at the advantages and disadvantages of *mixed* classes for Juniors.

ADVANTAGES OF MIXED GROUPS

Boys bring a slightly different mental attitude from that of girls to all that they are learning. A more all-round outlook is grasped when the learning group is mixed.

The more aggressive attitudes of boys are 'softened' when balanced by the different behaviour of girls. In the same way, the spiteful and 'catty' behaviour that can thrive in an all-girls group stands much less chance of survival in a mixed group. It is *not* more difficult to control mixed groups.

If boys and girls meet and do things together in a Christian context, they can learn a Christian attitude to members of the opposite sex. If this is left till adolescence, the teenagers' self-consciousness and rapidly developing awareness of the opposite sex will make it more difficult for boys and girls to treat one another in a natural, friendly and Christian way.

DISADVANTAGES OF MIXED GROUPS

Illustrative stories have to be carefully planned. Too many stories about girls will make the boys feel dissatisfied and vice versa—but a balance can be struck from week to week.

If the sexes are unevenly balanced and the children are divided into groups for any activity, one sex can feel swamped by the other. It may be better to have two mixed and two single-sexed classes rather than four classes, each consisting of five girls and two boys.

The considerations in the left-hand column *are* of more significance than those on the right. What appears on the right calls, however, for additional comment.

Stories that are *always* geared to the interests of boys—e.g., football—will soon make girls feel they are being overlooked. This does not mean that reference to football can *never* be made with a mixed group, but that one must also refer to something that girls will appreciate, just as a minister giving a sermon will include illustrations to appeal to men *and* to women. There is, of course, a vast area of experience common to both boys and girls from which illustrations can be drawn—pets, things that happen at school, family events, birthdays, and all the experience of joy and disappointment, of fear and eager anticipation, of guilt and forgiveness, of excitement and of anxiety. There are the sights which present themselves to children in their own neighbourhood or on television.

Leaders of groups which segregate the sexes sometimes fear that it would be more difficult to lead a mixed group, that boys ought to be led exclusively by men and girls by women. It *is* important for boys to know a Christian man whom they can respect and trust, lest they receive an impression that being a Christian is not for men. If, however, the leaders work together as a *team*, and the children get to know them all, there is no reason why the boys and girls, when divided into small 'classes' or groups, should not be taught by either a man or a woman. They *are* growing up in a mixed society, and we should be helping them to do so in a *Christian* way, not encouraging them to regard the opposite sex as strange beings with whom one does not mix. It is neither helpful nor wise to encourage competition between the sexes. They are intended to complement one another—not compete! Nor should we put a boy among the girls as a punishment. Our actions should not teach a sub-Christian view.

JUNIOR AND 'THE GANG'

By the time a child is nine or ten, he is wanting to conform to the standards and patterns of behaviour of others of his own age—and, usually, his own sex. When with them he may be cheeky to an adult just to make his friends admire his boldness. A child who is very amenable on his own can be very different when with the 'gang'. He may behave very differently when with them from the way he behaves at home. One member of the group will 'spark off' a reaction in another—and the teacher or leader of such a group has to deal with the group personality and not only with each child as an individual.

Here, in fact, is one of our difficulties. We need to treat each boy or girl in a group alike—and yet, to some extent, each requires to be treated as an individual. One child may need a lot of encouragement and drawing out, while another needs a firmer hand, a more determined (a cheerful and confident) tone of voice. We need then to understand:

- each boy or girl as an individual, different from everyone else;
- the characteristics common to children of this age-group and how they learn (this is taken up in chapter 5);
- the way boys and girls develop and behave differently at different ages;
- the leadership skills needed in controlling a group.

It is to this last need that we must now turn.

Chapter Three

LOOK OUT! CHILDREN!

The noise was deafening. The children had arrived at the hall before any of the leaders—a mistake on the leaders' part—and had taken control. When it was time to start, there was still some discussion about the 'right' hymn tune. From then on, things went from bad to worse. The atmosphere was wrong even when the children were quietened.

DEALING WITH A GROUP

What results when a group gets out of hand? Any children who do want to learn cannot do so because of the noise; the children feel that there are no limits to what they will be allowed to do, and their own insecurity because of this prompts them to behave even more badly; the teacher or leader feels anxious and possibly ashamed because he feels helpless, and then he reacts with hostility—and the battle is on. Children will enjoy such a trial of strength; it makes them feel bigger, stronger, and more independent of the adult world. We must not let this 'him versus us' situation arise, for the following reasons:

★ It is not consistent with the Gospel we are teaching, which is about a God of both love *and* righteousness, a God of order and not of chaos. We make a big mistake if we feel that we must tolerate any kind of behaviour because we represent the God who is love. We should no more be without standards, tolerant of anything, easy-going, prepared to ignore what is wrong, than He is. To allow a group of children to run wild when we are supposed to be in control will make it impossible for children to hear what we say because what we *are* will be speaking to them more loudly.

★ Good 'class control', as we might call it, matters. Children cannot learn with the atmosphere of warfare around them. Most will not *want* to learn when there is the exciting prospect of seeing how red in the face Miss X will grow, or how far Mr. Y can be provoked before he reacts in anger.

★ The children who are not happy about the situation, and who do not enjoy it, may well leave. They will feel insecure without the knowledge of how far they can go and without standards of behaviour which are *consistent*. It will not do to allow hymn-books to be thrown down one week and to insist on them being put carefully into a pile the next week.

★ For their own good, children need to develop good 'habits of work'—to do things in an orderly manner, to be punctual and hardworking, to put things away after using them, and so on. To allow children to behave differently is to train them in being inconsiderate to other people.

All this applies to *any* part of a Sunday School programme, whether we are acting as quiz master or helping children to find answers from the Bible about an event described there, whether we are leading in prayer or teaching a new chorus. It can happen in a week-night club or in a children's mission talk, at a party or on an outing. It can happen at any time when children are bored

Not . . . stone-like immobility

or rebellious—or when the person leading them is indecisive, afraid to be firm, or badly prepared so that there is a pause and children are left unoccupied.

But 'Good discipline is not to be thought of as meaning deathly silence and stone-like immobility. We do not measure it by noise or movement, but by the teacher's control of the learning situation and by his ability to carry or direct his class forward to the destination he has chosen. We must measure discipline not so much by the by-products but by the end-product—what has been learned . . . We may define good discipline as the creation and maintenance of such a relationship between teacher and class as shall make learning possible without interruption or distraction.'*

THE CAUSE OF THE TROUBLE?

Look back to the picture on p. 23. If all that was going on at a time when you were speaking to the children, what might be assumed about your teaching? Is it what children might call 'an SOS lesson' —same old stuff? Is it what someone else has described as a lesson with an uninteresting beginning, an insipid middle and an uninspiring ending?

Here is a list of some of the reasons for children getting restless and perhaps even out of hand.

1. Boredom—with the way the subject is being presented because it seems irrelevant to a child's life.
2. Boredom—because the language being used is not as simple and straightforward as that of a child. (Beware of 'special language' in prayer or in a version of the Bible that children do not fully understand.)
3. Boredom—because someone else is doing all the talking, and the child has nothing to do.
4. Boredom—because there is not enough variety and the same thing happens in almost the same order in the same way every time.
5. Boredom—because each separate item goes on for too long. Watch out for long hymns (sing selected verses only), and *never* have a prolonged period of chorus singing. Some children (older boys especially) really do *not* like singing.

There can be other reasons, too, of course . . .

Michael feels insecure and unhappy because of his parents' constant quarrelling. He needs to feel sure of *someone's* real concern

---

*J. R. Hill, in *Sunday School Teaching*.

and love for him. What truths about God are especially appropriate to his need? If he were in your group, how would you try to help him?

Caroline is full of resentment. 'It's not fair!' she's thinking. 'When Uncle Bob comes round he always has fun with us—and I've had to come *here* just as he was arriving. Think what I'm missing! Well, I'm not going to enjoy any of this!' Caroline may sulk—or she may take it out on the others around—leaders or children.

Stephen is apprehensively eyeing his Bible. 'She'll have us reading round again—and the others will laugh at me because I'm no good . . . I'll play up and show them I'm good at *something*.'

How could this situation have been avoided? Stephen may leave if he is *made* to read and feels he is an object of scornful pity or laughter.

Jane is tired of seeing all the attention go to her baby brother. Her mother has much less time for her—and she is feeling rather lost and in need of attention. On Sunday, she sets out to get attention in the only way she knows. She'd rather be in trouble than ignored.

SOME DO'S

1. **Do** be friendly—but firm.
2. **Do** be as courteous to children as you would be to adults. A 'please' and a 'thank you' are never out of place.
3. **Do** keep one step ahead of the children. Anticipate. John is looking inattentive and his hands is going into his pocket. Look him steadily in the eye so as to suggest by your glance, 'I *do* know what you're up to—and it's going to stop straight away.'
4. **Do** keep the children occupied. John needs not just a warning glance—but something else to do.
5. **Do** plan a programme that is varied and interesting, relevant to the children and geared to their abilities and needs.
6. **Do** be consistent. Treat children fairly and keep the same standards of behaviour from one week to the next, making it quite clear that you expect the boys and girls *always* to measure up to these standards.

SOME DON'T'S

1. **Don't** disguise an order as a question. 'Shall we sing hymn 147?' may provoke the answer 'No!' Say with confidence 'We'll now sing hymn 147'—your tone of voice suggesting that you have no doubt

that the children are going to be co-operative. There is no question of disobedience.

2. **Don't** make either threats which you cannot carry out or promises which you are unlikely to keep. If you do say, 'We'll have a new team chart next time,' make sure you keep your word. Write yourself a reminder if you are likely to forget, or ask children to remind you.

3. **Don't** laugh at the children or be sarcastic—but laugh with them, even if it is at yourself. A sense of humour is a great asset. Make sure that you stop laughing, however, before you want the children to do so. It is not so easy for them to control their laughter.

4. **Don't** be too anxious about being popular. The teacher who cannot be respected is not usually liked very much anyway.

5. **Don't** have favourites—or scapegoats (children on whom you look with suspicion immediately there is trouble).

6. **Don't** be authoritarian—a petty dictator barking out orders and ruling by fear. Being authoritative is a different matter. You have had authority delegated to you, and you should not be afraid to use it, but should show decisiveness and a quiet confidence.

GETTING THE RIGHT ATMOSPHERE

Here are some phrases that children might hear. Imagine yourself in their place, and decide which phrases would create the right attitude of mind and help you to want to learn, to enjoy what is being done and to be a co-operative member of the group.

1 I told you so.
2. I want to see how well you can do it.
3. We haven't time now. You've wasted too much time already.
4. Thank you, John. You read that very well.
5. You're almost right. Can anyone help?
6. Sit *still*! And *stop* talking!
7. If I've told you once, I've told you a dozen times.
8. Let's see which team can be ready first.
9. Why can't you behave like Mr. Jones' group?
10. That's very good, Elizabeth. Let's put it up on our wallchart.

Numbers 2, 4, 5, 8 and 10 are the remarks of someone who is encouraging and sympathetic, someone who understands a child's need to feel appreciated even if his answers are not 100% correct. The other remarks suggest someone who is impatient, unsympathetic, intolerant and unable to keep order.

Never compare one group of children unfavourably with another (see phrase 9). The speaker there is obviously a very different person from Mr. Jones, and it is he (or she) who is at fault, not the children. They will reflect to some extent the person in charge; they will be noisy and excitable if *he* is noisy and excitable. They will be well-controlled if *he* is calm and self-controlled.

LEADERSHIP

His task is to *lead* the children, much as a captain leads his football team. He is to be one with them, rather than an onlooker shouting instructions from the touch-line, because he, too, is a learner—a disciple—of Christ's. *Spiritually, his leadership will be effective only if he himself is led by Christ and subject to His discipline.*

Such a teacher may, in fact, prefer the term 'leader', because it suggests that the class (or 'group', which may be a better term) belongs as much to the children as to the adult in charge. Think of the way in which a children's TV programme 'belongs' to its viewers as much as to those who compère the programme. We can learn from the approach of these men and women as long as we remember that they visualize the individual child sitting before the TV set. They do not have to take into account the way children will react *as a group*. In such a situation the leader must clearly *lead*. It is a big mistake to try to be 'one of the boys' with children; they want you to be yourself—in clothing and manner. They are immature emotionally as well as in other ways, and need a leader whom they can respect, rely on, and obey. It is generally better to be called Miss X, Mrs. Y or Mr. Z—children do not easily identify a leadership role with someone they call Jenny, Chris or Uncle Bob.

EMERGENCY ACTION

No air-line would ignore safety regulations and simply provide life-jackets and instructions to passengers on what to do in an emergency. The first thing to do about trouble is to *prevent* it, and this is what this chapter has been all about. If we understand children, prepare activities that are suited to their age and ability and linked to their interests and needs, and know how to lead them, most trouble will be prevented.

Occasionally, however, an aircraft crashes—and emergency action is needed . . . .

Miss Elliot is taking emergency action with an offending child,

37

Peter, who has been causing trouble for some time. Now he is ready to jerk Christine's chair away as soon as she goes to sit down. Miss Elliot is well aware of this and fixes him with her eye while she goes on talking to Christine. Peter gazes back, unabashed—and keeps his hand outstretched towards the chair.

Next, Miss Elliot asks a direct question: 'Peter, what do *you* think Christine could add to this prayer picture? Who else is there to pray for?'

Peter really is in a rebellious mood—or else he has something he's holding against Christine. He answers—and keeps his hand outstretched towards the chair. No, he has *not* forgotten his original intention.

Christine turns towards her chair. 'Peter!' says Miss Elliot, a note of warning in her voice—but he has already pulled the chair away, and Christine is on the floor.

Peter has ignored every warning signal. His behaviour cannot be overlooked. If Miss Elliot does nothing, how will Christine feel? What will she think?

Miss Elliot has got to do something. Which of these possibilities do you consider best?

1. 'Peter! Outside this minute—and don't come back in till you're really sorry.'
2. 'Since you're behaving like a baby, you'd better go and join the babies. Go on—go and tell Mrs. Wood I thought you'd be better with her five-year-olds.'
3. 'That's enough of that. Come and sit next to me.'
4. 'We can't have one person spoiling things for everybody else—that wouldn't be fair. Put your chair here—just in front of me—and I'll talk to you afterwards. And any more of that kind of behaviour and you'll lose a team point. Now let's see if you can put the words of this memory text in the right order. Here you are.'

How well did you use your imagination?
The first possibility can look to a child like an admission of defeat—and it may be that! It also raises a number of questions: Does 'outside' produce a number of other exciting possibilities—like peering through a window and making faces at the children, or playing football with a stone in the yard? Could it put temptation in Peter's way—coat pockets to rifle or playing truant for the rest of the time? What would happen if Peter dashed out and into the

path of oncoming traffic when his parents thought him safely in Miss Elliot's care? Is he going to hang around outside in winter without a coat, get thoroughly chilled, and bring his mother's wrath down upon Miss Elliot's head? Is he going to be a nuisance to other teachers, a distraction to other children? Is he going to come back in and 'play to the gallery' with a great show of mock penitence—and then see if Miss Elliot will send him out again when he next misbehaves?

This does not mean that there will never be a time when it is right to send a boy out. In some areas there will be children who are against all authority, largely because of their background and upbringing—and some of these may come to a Sunday School or church club. There *may* even be occasions when, for the sake of other children, one boy (or girl) has to be told he may not come again unless he is willing to behave as he should. Such action must, of course, be fully explained to the parents. But back to Peter—who is just a normal child, not one requiring special measures.

Miss Elliot's second possible course of action is even worse. Put yourself in Mrs. Wood's place. She has enough to do without having Peter added to it all. *His* version of why he has been sent in to her may puzzle Mrs. Wood—or even be aimed at showing off to the five-year-olds and making them laugh. Why should Mrs. Wood's programme be broken into with this interruption? Think of Peter, too. How is he likely to feel towards Miss Elliot? Of course he may *enjoy* being with the younger ones and able to help—and choose to misbehave again!

Peter should certainly be moved away from Christine in order to prevent further trouble. Even if *he* stops provoking her, *she* may try to get her own back on him. Miss Elliot is still asking for trouble, however, if she seats Peter beside her. She cannot easily see any child in that position. The child sitting there knows it—and also sees the possibilities there are in *facing* the other children. Again, use your imagination and think what Peter could do . . . this is learning to anticipate trouble and prevent it.

The fourth possibility is the one that has most to commend it. Look at what it contains:

1. *A reason why Peter's behaviour is unacceptable:* 'We can't have one person spoiling things for everybody else—that wouldn't be fair.' Children of Junior age are often more co-operative when they

can see a reason for what an adult is demanding. Miss Elliot is thinking of the other children—and Peter is a minority. She is being reasonable and fair.

2. *Action to remove Peter from the source of temptation:* 'Put your chair here—just in front of me.' Away from Christine, he may behave differently. He is told to sit *in front* of Miss Elliot, where she can see him, not beside her, where he could distract others and escape her notice.

3. *The clear implication that Peter's action is not one that can be ignored:* 'I'll talk to you afterwards.' Miss Elliot must remember to do so! She will tell him what she thinks of his action—when no one else is around. Christine will not be there to gloat over him, and his friends will not be there for him to show off. He cannot play to the gallery and is more likely to take Miss Elliot's words to heart.

4. *A warning which is not an empty threat:* 'Any more of that kind of behaviour and you'll lose a team point.' Having said that she will take off that point if he disregards her warning, she must do as she has said. To ignore further misbehaviour and say 'I'll give you one more chance' is to suggest to the whole group that they can do as they like without any fear of repercussions. (If the team system had not been in use, a warning that she would speak to his parents would have been a suitable alternative.)

5. *An incentive for a change in behaviour.* Peter's team will add their warning looks to Miss Elliot's if they see him on the verge of mis-behaviour. They do not want him losing a point for the team.

6. *Something else to occupy Peter:* 'Now let's see if you can put the words of this memory text in the right order.' He is given something else to do to occupy him.

7. *A change of tone to indicate that there is no war to wage.* Miss Elliot does not keep on and on! Peter has a chance to put the whole thing behind him and make a fresh start.

8. *An opportunity to gain praise and appreciation.* If Peter can sort out the words of the memory text, he will receive Miss Elliot's 'Well done!' and feel the glow of satisfaction at having achieved something. (The activity should be something that he will do fairly quickly and easily.) If his earlier behaviour was an attempt to gain attention, he will now have found a better way to do it.

Of course, Miss Elliot may not be able to do all this *every* time Peter behaves badly. Nor will she be able to think all this out between the moment when Christine lands on the floor and the second or two later when she must do something about it. The ability to take the right action, without having to think too long about it, grows with experience—but thinking beforehand what one *would* do in a certain situation can be a great help.

Picture the most difficult child in your group and think of something which he or she *might* do. Now work out what would be the best action to take.

Chapter Four

WHAT ARE WE TRYING TO DO?

Sunday School may be enjoyed—or endured!

A school-teacher was looking through the latest literary efforts of her class—stories called, 'How I caught a . . .' Alan had chosen to write on 'How I caught a cold'. The story—a true one regrettably—was about what he called his 'Sunday Class'. It was clear that he had gone there reluctantly, but had at least met his best friend when he arrived. Then . . .

'Time dragged slowly by,' he wrote. 'My friend sneezed—right in my face—and my Sunday Class teacher told him to be quiet. Time dragged slowly by. Then my friend sneezed again. "Stop that," I said. "Will you be quiet?" said our teacher. Time dragged slowly by . . .'

We need not finish the sad tale. Alan caught a cold—but the hour's programme seems to have had little effect other than boring at least one of the children. What *was* wrong with this 'Sunday Class'?

We cannot possibly know the answer to that, but Alan's story would surely have shocked his Sunday Class teacher had she seen it. I wonder if she and the other members of the staff there had ever tried to see their Sunday Class as the *children* must have seen it?

A CHILD'S EYE VIEW

Here is what Alan might tell us about his Sunday School. Decide which facts are 'essentials' that should not be altered.

1. We meet on Sundays.
2. We have a kind of service first.
3. The Superintendent takes that.
4. After the service part we go to our classes.
5. The boys are in different classes from the girls.
6. Our teachers talk to us and then we often have to draw something.

7. We learn about God.

Now let's take each one in turn.

WHEN?

Does a 'Sunday School' *have* to take place on Sunday? What is the the most important thing about a Sunday School? Is it its name—or is it what happens there? If local circumstances make it advisable, why should it not take place as a week-night 'club', or on a Saturday morning?

WHAT AND WHY?

'We learn about God.' Here *is* an essential. We are not aiming to keep boys and girls entertained, or off the streets, or out of their parents' way. We are not seeking merely to educate them. We want them to come to know that God exists, and that He loves them, and that . . . we could go on with a very long list of facts.

There is more to it than facts, however. Here is a good aim for our work, based on 2 Tim. 3. 15–17.

● That children may learn the basic truth about God and man. ('From childhood you have been acquainted with the sacred writings . . . All scripture is inspired by God and profitable for teaching . . .')

● That they may be led to salvation through faith in Jesus Christ ('. . . The sacred writings are able to instruct you for salvation through faith in Christ Jesus.')

● That they may have wrong ways of life corrected and be instructed in right standards. ('. . . Scripture is . . . profitable for teaching, for reproof, for correction, and for training in righteousness . . .')

● That they may grow up to be men of God, equipped for 'good work of every kind', ready to play their full part in the church and in society. ('. . . that the man of God may be complete, equipped for every good work.')

HOW?

'We have a kind of service first. . . . After the service part, we go to our classes. The boys are in different classes from the girls. . . . Our teachers talk to us and then we often have to draw something.'

It is a familiar pattern—perhaps too familiar.

Sunday School does not *have* to be a service followed by a lesson.

Boys do not *have* to be in different classes from girls. Lessons do not *have* to be a monotonous 'You sit still and listen while I do the talking' monologue, followed—if there is time—by letting children draw the Bible story for the sake of them having had something to do.

WHO?

There is no reason either why the Superintendent or departmental leader *must* take everything except a lesson, or why those in his team of teachers should always each take a whole lesson with a small group of children and never do anything else. The next chapter will give some alternatives.

WHY 'SUNDAY SCHOOL'?

In a country where 'school' is something to which adults do not go (for the word 'college' is more frequently used at the higher education levels), 'Sunday School' can imply something to grow out of, along with children's clothes and childish games.

This is *not* the impression we want to give about the Christian faith. For this reason the name 'Sunday School' is one that is better dropped.

Various names are often used instead but let us make sure that we choose one that will appeal to the children *and* to the parents. We must not give the impression of being still in a bygone era, even if parents find it hard to drop the phrase they are most used to.

Once we are not using the word 'school', we may well ask, 'Then why use the other words associated with it—teacher, class, or lesson?'

superintendent	leader	
class	group	Which list do you think
teacher	group leader	you would prefer if you
lesson	group-time	were a Junior child?

THE PARENTS' VIEW

Mrs. Smith and Mrs. Brown are talking in the supermarket.

'My Susan wants to start going to—what do they call it?— Explorers? Your Caroline goes, doesn't she?'

'*Yes. Well, I think it does them good. I'm not religious myself— but I'd like Caroline to have some sort of faith. Growing-up's got its problems these days.*'

'Yes—life was a lot more straightforward for you and me. I can see I'm going to be worried out of my life about Susan when she's a few years older.'

'*Mind you, I wouldn't want Caroline to become **too** religious—but I don't think that's very likely. We're not a family that goes to church.*'

'Nor are we. Well, some people are interested in one thing and some in another. I'd like Susan to *know* about church and all that; she can make up her own mind when she's older. I wouldn't *make* her go but she really seems to want to.'

'*Well, Caroline seems to enjoy it. There's quite a fuss when we want to take her round to my mother's for the day on Sunday. I think*' *it's rather different from what Sunday School was like in my young days.'*

REACHING THE FAMILY

Mrs. Smith and Mrs. Brown are like thousands of others—without Christ, but wanting to live what they would call 'a decent life' and thinking that this is what it means to be a Christian. They believe in God in a vague, general sense, but have never come into a real relationship with Him through personal faith in Christ as Saviour and Lord. They do not really know what it is all about. They need to get to know Him through people whose lives have a different quality of life—eternal life—because they have peace with God, forgiveness, true security, joy and strength in Him, and a transforming love-relationship with God. Above all else, they need to *see* the real thing, not just hear about it. They need to meet the risen Christ in us.

Anything we can do to let them see Christ in us is therefore important. The church that is awake to the opportunities of meeting men and women, boys and girls, through its 'Sunday School' work will plan 'open' meetings when parents can come and see an ordinary Sunday session in action, family occasions when the whole family can join together either for a special service or for some other activity, parents' evenings (baby-sitters provided) when practical help can be given by a Christian doctor, or teacher, or by someone able to help with family problems. (Further ideas for contacting families are given in *Today's Children, Tomorrow's Church*.)

EVANGELISM AND TEACHING

'Do you think I have failed if I haven't given a 'Gospel challenge' at the end of *every* lesson?' asks a teacher; 'Suppose during this next week someone decides to leave and never hears the Gospel again? Suppose one of them runs in front of a bus? Should I make sure every lesson ends with a challenge to commit one's life to Christ?'

Miss Robinson was puzzled. To her, it did not seem quite right to tug every lesson round until it turned into an evangelistic appeal—and she was quite right. We should certainly pray that boys and girls will make the *appropriate response* to the teaching we are giving, but if, for example, our aim one week is to teach that God can be anywhere, the response we shall pray for is that wherever

46

children go they may have the realization that there is no place where God cannot be with them. This is not likely to be a 'lesson' which will bring a child the final step 'from darkness to light' (Acts 26. 18), but it may well take a child one step nearer. Since, however, the Holy Spirit's work of conviction and drawing to Christ is His work and not ours, He will not be bound by our preconceived ideas—and a boy or girl may come to real personal faith and be born again of the Spirit as a result of teaching that is *not* what we would call 'evangelistic'.

To give a 'Gospel appeal' week after week is likely to lead either to a hardness and inability to respond, or to spurious 'conversions' which are not the real thing at all. Miss Robinson needs to remember that her group consists of Linda and Carol, Tracey and Sue, Kevin and Peter, Mike and Gary—each an individual, each one different, and each at a different point spiritually. The Holy Spirit knows how they are going to respond to Christ and when. Miss Robinson's teaching must be seen as working *towards* the full achievement of the aim given on p. 43, although the children may have several teachers before the Sunday School and Bible Class can say that their task has been complete . . . and there will probably be some who do not come to a real faith in Christ at all. It is unlikely that *every* child in a class group will come to 'salvation through faith in Jesus Christ' during the year in which he is taught by a particular teacher—although it is possible. One of the great advantages given to those who teach in a Sunday School is that there is time to see a steady development and a deepening understanding on the part of the child. The staff of the *entire* Sunday School/Bible Class/ church can work as a team to nurture the child; there is no need to try to telescope all the teaching into a short period. We do not need to attempt to teach 'the whole counsel of God' (Acts 20. 27) *in one lesson*—but each lesson should make a *single* contribution to this whole.

SYSTEMATIC TEACHING

This means that the teaching can be seen as taking place over the course of some years. It should be based on a syllabus which takes proper consideration of the experiences and needs of each age-group, and which builds upon the teaching given at an earlier stage. It can be very boring for a child to hear the same Bible stories year after year, just because there is no syllabus being followed.

47

WHAT OF OUR INFLUENCE?

Children need not only to know how Christ behaved and what he did; they must see who Christ is and what He does today. The teaching that is also a teaching-evangelism shows Christ alive in our world, able to meet *our* needs; He is not just the Jesus of history. The Holy Spirit still speaks to boys and girls, as well as to men and women, through the life of a regenerate, Spirit-filled teacher, who reveals Christ as much in what he *is* as through what he *says*. We must not forget that God needs to be able to use the personal life of the teacher as well as the lesson material that is presented. However relevant our teaching—and it *must* throw light upon the child's world—it must be matched by our living. Only thus can teaching work towards and include evangelism.

How easy it is to be so preoccupied with the week-by-week details that we lose sight of the ultimate purpose of it all! Sunday arrives—and it may be one of the busiest days in our week. The sad result could be a teacher who rushes in at the last minute, leaves as soon as possible after the children have been dismissed, and is satisfied if all goes smoothly without disciplinary problems. If this happens week after week, a child's own particular need may not be recognized, and it will not occur to the boy or girl that his teacher might be interested and willing to talk over things that are on his or her mind. No friendly relationship will exist to inspire confidence or encourage the sharing of thoughts and feelings.

INTRODUCING CHILDREN TO CHRIST

The teacher who makes and uses opportunities to get to know the children better will be the one who is most likely to find the children ready for what is often termed 'personal work'. Personal work does not mean acting as a spiritual midwife and having no further care for the 'babe in Christ'. It includes all personal conversations with an individual before and after his conversion.

When talking about a spiritual subject to the child the teacher can range among the wealth of Biblical material which he knows is familiar to that boy or girl. He can find illustrations among the surroundings and situations of that child's everyday life. He is like a housewife whose larder is so well-stocked that she is able to choose what to give to a unexpected guest instead of deciding, 'It will have to be beans on toast.'

The teacher who is building on teaching given perhaps over some time, and who knows the child and his background, is less likely to make the mistake of taking a well-tried but adult formula and using *that* with the child who wants to know more about becoming a real Christian. There will be no 'Here is the ABC of the Gospel; do this . . . this . . . and this—and you're there!'

Instead, he will so question and talk with the child, sensitive both to him and to the leading of the Holy Spirit, that he can make a careful and thorough enquiry into the child's understanding of repentance and faith. He will understand what the cost of being a Christian is likely to be for that *particular* child, and will not present something that is true for an adult or teenager but not for a child. Nor will he be so vague about what it means to give one's life to Christ that the child thinks his life can go on exactly as before, with no turning away from sin and no willingness to obey Christ as one's Lord and King. Such a teacher will know where to draw the line between giving the kind of instruction that implies. You will be a Christian if you just do these three things' (as though it were all a matter of human response), and between giving so little practical instruction that the child either cannot grasp *how* he comes and commits his life to One whom he cannot see, or believes that there is nothing for *him* to do at all (as though it were entirely a matter of divine calling, requiring no response from man).

It is, of course, essential to avoid any atmosphere, language, tone of voice, or question, that will put pressure upon a child to make the response he thinks you are wanting from him. The greater the teacher's influence upon a child, the greater will be the possibility of an unreal profession of faith, one made solely to please the teacher.

Other forms of 'pressure' that we might not recognize as such are the request to 'put up your hand in the next prayer if you want to ask Jesus into your life', or to 'come to me afterwards if you want to know more about becoming a Christian and I will give you a booklet.' Here, emotion or the response of a friend, or the prospect of a free gift, can pressurize a child into making a response that is not a true commitment in repentance and faith.

Chapter Five

NOW I'M A TEACHER . . .

A REAL TEACHER?

Michael sat very upright in his chair as his mother came through the classroom room with the headmistress. 'Some of you have seen Michael's mummy before,' said Mrs. Freeman, 'but perhaps you didn't know she is a teacher.'

'What? A *real* teacher?' asked one dumb-founded child, who couldn't imagine anyone being both mother and teacher.

What other tasks do *you* combine with that of teaching and leading Junior children—shop assistant, housewife, student, secretary, school-girl? Few of those whom God calls to serve Him by teaching boys and girls each Sunday are also called to teach children from Monday to Friday. Do the children compare us with their 'real' teachers? Many will—especially if we use the word 'teacher' rather than 'leader'.

Let's remember that we are not *trying* to do the same job. The day school teacher faces the task of educating the whole child. We too, face the whole child—not just a soul to be won. Religious education in school is not intended to bring a child into a saving relationship with God. In some schools, the teaching will conflict with the teaching we give.

WHAT DO CHILDREN EXPECT?

'I'd like you to write down what *you* think Sunday School teachers ought to do and be like,' I said. 'It's your own ideas I want—and be quite honest. You needn't put your name on your paper.'

The children were enthusiastic. They knew I was writing a book for Sunday School teachers, and liked the idea of making their own contribution.

Let's look at some of their expectations . . . and then at ourselves.

'I think Sunday School teachers should be kind and good. They should be stern with the people who play around when someone is telling us about the Bible . . .'

'They should be kind, and they should understand us . . .'

'Sunday School teachers should be kind to their pupils, and have games at times and be fun (and strict at times) . . .'

'I think that Sunday School teachers should want to teach children about Jesus and God and be willing to spare their time to it . . .'

'I think that they should let the children do a special play in front of the people in church every 4—6 weeks and also encourage the children to go to church. Sunday School teachers should give Bible quizzes quite often to help the children remember what they have learnt . . .'

'The teachers should help children to understand the Bible and answer as many questions as they can . . .'

'They should explain things about the Bible that you don't understand . . .'

'I think that Sunday School teachers should have a good idea of what they are talking about . . .'

WHAT DO YOU KNOW?

Yes, they expect us to know what we are talking about, and this means—an unpopular word—work! Of course we must prepare thoroughly, giving ourselves time to discover what the Bible actually says and what it can mean both for us and for the child today. It will often help to read a Bible passage in more than one version. Above all, we need to ask for the teaching of the Holy Spirit, the author of the Book, to be given to us, and if our preparation does not include prayer and thinking over the passage with our minds open to God for *Him* to teach us, we have not prepared adequately at all. Head knowledge is important—but it will have little effect upon the children if they do not see us living by it ourselves. We must know what we are talking about—in our own experience. Study of the Bible in our preparation needs, too, to be accompanied by regular, daily Bible reading if we are to know when God is speaking to us.

KNOWING GOD

Even more important, we must know whom we are talking about.

We cannot bring a child into a living, personal relationship with Jesus Christ if we do not know Him ourselves as Saviour and Lord. And when we can say we know Him, do we go on to see that our relationship with Him grows and deepens into a rich experience, filling our lives with love and joy and the power of the Holy Spirit, drawing others to Christ? We cannot teach others what we do not know ourselves—and we want children not just to know the salvation He gives to the one who turns in repentant faith to Him, but to glorify Him in a life that shows Him to others.

KNOWING HOW CHILDREN LEARN

We must know our subject and we must know God for ourselves—but we must also know children, and understand how they learn. We have already considered how we can get to know individual boys and girls and what are the general characteristics of the Junior age-group. What else do we need to understand about them?

Interest, experience and discovery

It is no good just *expecting* a child to 'pay attention'; we must 'buy' his attention by offering something that is of interest to him. The teacher who begins, 'Now today we're going to have the story of Moses in the bulrushes' is not likely to have the children sitting on the edges of their chairs in eager anticipation! They *know* the story of baby Moses—or think they do—and may well be wondering what it has to do with them, living in a very different world. It can seem remote, unreal and irrelevant . . . and yet it is not so at all—if we begin to consider what Moses' family learned about God from all that happened to them. Think of Moses' sister, Miriam. Does her experience have anything to say to the children? Here is another way of introducing the story, one which does not immediately tell the children who the story is about, but captures their interest and appeals to their curiosity:

'The little girl crouched down in the tall, waving grasses by the river. The grasses tickled her bare arms and made her want to wriggle—but she knew she must keep still; no one must notice her. Then suddenly . . . shh! There were voices . . . and they were getting closer, laughing and chattering. "Oh God," she prayed, "Please don't let them see me. I must find out what happens if they see the basket"—and anxiously she looked at the gently bobbing water of the river Nile.'

Let us look at the advantages of beginning this way:

1. Every child has had the experience of hiding and not wanting to be discovered—so this introduction helps those listening to identify themselves with the girl, Miriam. It reminds them of their own experience.

2. Everyone enjoys a story, and this one begins with something happening—and the children are interested.

3. The story is building up rapidly to a note of suspense. The children are curious about what is going to happen.

4. If the story-teller uses a very quiet tone of voice, as though also identifying with Miriam as she keeps—oh, so still . . . the children listening will also be very quiet and still. (This can be very desirable at the start of one's teaching!)

Other introductions can, of course, make use of other ways in which children learn.

Stephen's interest was gripped the moment his Sunday School teacher began asking questions about the children's favourite games. He was now goalkeeper in the school football team—and still a little sore about the goal he had failed to stop but felt sure should not have allowed by the referee. 'That boy *was* off-side!' he protested.

'So you think rules ought to be kept, do you?' his Sunday School teacher now asked.

'Well, of course!' he affirmed.

'But suppose you had been the boy who scored—not the goal-keeper? Would you still have said the rule should be kept?'

'I'm not sure,' he admitted.

'But a rule's a rule,' said Susan. 'If one side has to keep the rules, so has the other. It wouldn't be fair otherwise.'

'But why have rules at all?' asked the teacher . . . and the conversation went on until they came to consider *God's* rules.

Stephen was learning. His interest had been captured, he was using his own experience to enable him to think and understand, and he was reaching out to new ideas.

It is only by experience that the thinking of a small child develops and concepts are formed. What does a child learn from this?

One such experience is not going to be enough to teach him:

(a) that a table top always rests on the table legs;

(b) that a table top is hard;

(c) that he is taller than the table leg.

Through this experience, *and* that of sitting in a high chair at the table and seeing its use, *and* many other experiences of seeing and touching tables, the young child forms a concept of what a table is. Through more than one experience of banging his head, he learns to judge his own height and that of any space in which he wishes to move.

All our concepts are built up in this way—and this is what makes it so difficult to teach a child that God can be trusted if his experience of life has taught him only about untrustworthiness. If he has found his parents to be unreliable and inconsistent, he will find it very hard to believe that God is any different. Such a child's concept of authority is of something that is not always fair but can sometimes be placated or persuaded to a change of mind.

In teaching children, we need always to bear in mind that the child's experience is still very limited, and that there are, therefore, many adult experiences, emotions and thoughts which will necessarily be beyond his understanding. We must be careful in our choice of Bible stories, and in how we use the stories we do select, for this very reason, and not use stories which introduce ideas quite beyond a child's understanding—however much this has been done in the past.

Abraham's offering of his son, Isaac, is a good example here. A child's idea of what a good father should be like has no place in it for killing one's son, no matter who gives the command. A child's reasoning, even if not thought out consciously, is 'If God told Abraham to do that, I don't like Him.' The child is, after all, emotionally bound to his own parents and physically dependent on them, too. He could not bear the thought of *his* father preparing to sacrifice him, so his ability to understand the story is blocked by his own experience and emotional reaction. He is too young for that story, even though he can understand the facts of it. In trying to give him one idea—absolute obedience, for example—we unconsciously convey another. The child gains an impression which is a complete distortion of the truth: that God is cruel and unjust.

Some would use this story to symbolize the substitutionary aspect of the death of Christ: just as God showed Abraham a ram, caught in the thicket by his horns, to sacrifice instead, so He Himself provided the Lamb of God to die in our place. We may understand this imagery and be able to make the jump from 'just as' to 'so also', but how many of our Juniors will be able to make the same mental leaps? A few of the oldest and brightest, with the background of a good Christian home, may possibly be completely 'with us', but even they may merely understand the words and be accepting what they are told without really understanding the spiritual truth which we think we are conveying. The fact, is, children cannot make the mental jumps that we make. *In telling a Bible story, we must always ask ourselves, 'What did this mean to the people to whom this first happened?' The answer to **that** question is what we should teach from that story.*

Let's take the restoring of sight to Bartimaeus (Mark 10. 46–52) as an example. What did it all mean *to Bartimaeus*? Surely what he discovered was the compassion and power of the Son of God and the importance of faith? When we use the story in our teaching, one of these truths must be our reason for taking that particular incident. Adults may be able to jump from the physical blindness and restored sight of Bartimaeus to our being blinded by Satan from perceiving spiritual things and needing to be given spiritual sight—but children should not be expected to make this jump. Bartimaeus did not learn that day a lesson about spiritual blindness and his need of a Saviour from sin. The child can be helped to learn what Bartimaeus learned, and these are important truths for a child to learn. It is far better to use the Bible in this way with children than to spiritualize the stories it contains.

IDENTIFICATION—DRAMA

In reading story books, Juniors often have one question in mind as they read the first few pages: 'Who am I going to be in this book?' They are seeking to identify themselves with one character, and so 'experience' all that happens through that person. With Bible stories, too, there is often a desire to identify oneself with the hero or heroine—for this is another way in which children learn. In their play, we often see them acting out situations as they envisage them in the adult world—although these situations may appear to us to be widely over-dramatized!

Can we use the delight they find in such play to help them learn about God and what He has taught us through the Bible? 'Not me—not with my class anyway!' you may be murmuring. For most of us, it's no great loss to the world that we did *not* go on the stage! We have never had the least desire to set the theatrical world on fire.

We may have looked askance at everything to do with drama, and seen a great gulf fixed between 'us' and 'them'.

And now come suggestions about letting children act! We try . . . and it's a dismal failure!

'These children don't like acting' is one conclusion we may come to. Or perhaps it's 'I'm no good at this.'

Most children, once they've got into the way of it, enjoy acting but some really don't. They are too shy, too self-conscious, or afraid of looking foolish. We need to understand this and *never* single out such children. We can help them to gain confidence, however. It is possible that they have been over-criticised, made to feel inadequate, or had too much expected of them. Understanding this will help us to deal with the basic problem, not just with a symptom—dislike of acting.

If, of course, the group is verging on adolescence, the natural self-consciousness that accompanies this stage of growing-up may be the cause of any widespread dislike . . . and it is simply better in this case not to use drama as a teaching tool with such a group.

The fault, however, may be with us, and some practical tips may be of help.

★ Be enthusiastic and appear confident, however you feel.

★ Do not tell children what to say or give them words written down and expect them to turn from parrots into lively actors and actresses. Dialogues can be read, if the children are good enough readers—

but do not expect Juniors to be able to act at the same time. Forget about acting with words until the children are well-used to acting through mime and able to add their own words impromptu.

★ Make most use of drama when the whole group can be involved and can have some action to do. Either tell a story yourself while children mime, or get a good reader (prepared beforehand) to read the passage, pausing where appropriate, or accompany actions with an appropriate tambourine beat or gramophone record.

★ Encourage your actors to express feelings as they act—tiredness, surprise, doubt, joy, fear, etc. This will help them to come closer to the deeper truths in the story they are thinking about and acting.

★ If you want a group to act a whole story, let them find out which characters are needed and what each should do and say. Ask questions, so that they plan the scenes. They are not human puppets for you to move around and instruct with, 'Now say . . .'. When they have planned a scene, let them rehearse it but encourage them to work fast—for a maximum of two to three minutes. Let them then make their own suggestions for how it could be improved. Do not expect children to enjoy *watching* these first attempts. If children are going to watch at all and not take part themselves, they need to be presented with something thought out and prepared. Remember that the value of acting as an aid to learning is that it helps *those who take part* rather than those who watch.

★ Keep a few items for dressing-up in a large box or bag. Curtains, towels, old dressing-gowns, a cardboard crown and sword, a few lengths of tape and some safety pins, will help children's imagination. Remember, however, that children can work without any props— after a quick demonstration by their teacher!

Acting is worthwhile . . . and a lot of mime can be done in a very confined space and without being noisy and distracting to nearby groups. Other children will not see if you make use of teaching screens.

Imagination

Of course, it calls for imagination—but children usually have plenty of that! The following introduction to a lesson on Christ's triumphant entry into Jerusalem shows one way in which imagination may be used:

'Suppose someone very important (take a suitable local example— e.g., in the UK, the Queen) came to your town—what would happen?

Let the children describe the band that might play, the decorations, the people lining the streets, etc. Suppose you were standing there on the pavement as the Queen went past, what would you do? Why do you think people cheer when the Queen goes by? Help the children discover that the cheering is a way of showing the loyalty and love that people have for the Queen. It's something they naturally want to do when they have a suitable opportunity. This can lead on to helping the children to imagine themselves in Jerusalem when Christ rode in upon a donkey in accordance with the prophecy in Zech. 9. 9, and was welcomed as the longed-for Messiah.'

Another use of children's imaginative ability in our teaching lies in the simplest visual aids we can use. The beautifully-produced artist's idea of a Bible story is not necessarily a good visual aid, as it leaves no room for the imagination. Pictures of Jesus can be a real disappointment to children whose imagination had shown them something more wonderful. Our own simply-drawn 'stick-men' or 'pin-men' are readily clothed and brought to life by the child's imagination—and they can be drawn quickly as the story progresses, which gives another advantage over the picture that shows only one moment in the story.

Inspiring children to use *their* imagination is, of course, partly a matter of using our own imagination first, especially when we are telling a story—but that is a subject for chapter 9.

Suggestibility and intuition

Children are very suggestible and learn not only from *what* is said but from *how* it is said. In teaching about the return of the Lord Jesus Christ, for example, a lot can be conveyed to children by a note of joy and expectancy in one's voice as one talks of the wonder and thrill the Christian will experience at His coming. This is an example of a time when we should not be afraid of letting emotion come into our voices. There is a difference between putting emotional pressure on children and letting them see that what we teach means a very great deal to us and is no mere string of words.

Our attitudes and reactions carry their own message. The solemn teacher who no shows sign of having any sense of humour may be unconsciously suggesting to children that following Christ is a joyless business. The one who wears a perpetually worried look may be giving the impression that trust in God is useless. The too easy-going suggests, without being aware of it, that standards do not have to be held very rigidly; God will overlook our misdemeanours just as he or she is doing.

The room, too, always conveys its own message. Is it dilapidated, untidy, dingy and cheerless? Has the framed text on the wall been there for the last fifty years? No—the text itself is not out-of-date, but what about brown, mock-Gothic lettering and that lily entwined around it? Is the general impression one of the Christian faith being something for a bygone age? What about wall-pictures of Bible stories, produced many years in the past? Is the style of painting one that would strike today's children as 'old-fashioned'? Such things suggest that what is taught in this place is also for a past age, irrelevant to today, and not worth bothering about. If we do *not* bother about cleanliness and the general appearance of our meeting-place, we dishonour the Lord. Surely time and money must be found that this may be put right! And as the Sunday School *is* a part of the church and not a separate organization, let us see that the church *as a whole*—not just those whom it has called to represent them among the children—sees its financial responsibility here.

The impression conveyed to children by the place in which they meet is not, of course, only a matter of how the room looks. There needs to be the right 'atmosphere' for learning and worship. Music can help (see chapter 12), and so can flowers, charts produced by the children, colourful modern pictures and something—different each week—to attract the attention and interest of those who arrive early. It is essential that teachers or leaders arrive there before the children, so that they are able to create the right atmosphere. If they arrive *after* the children have made the room a place for chasing around, shouting, even fighting, it will be very difficult to bring about a different atmosphere.

Children are very suggestible to anything that stirs their emotions—and these, it must be remembered, are not the matured emotions of an adult. A child's emotions are easily roused. We know, for example, how quickly they can become over-excited . . . and how they over-react and it often ends in tears. We need to act responsibly here and take care *not* to 'work them up' and get them excited . . . and then ask for a response to the claims of Christ. Such a response can be merely human and not the work of the Holy Spirit in the child. It was 'emotional', not in this case because we made an emotional appeal—but because we had previously raised the child's emotional 'pitch'.

Repetition—and variety

One experience of this kind may not be enough—but if he bangs his head in this way repeatedly, he will learn to look up before hoisting himself to his feet.

Repetition is a valuable aid to learning—*but it must be meaningful.* Many of us learned things 'by heart' in the past and have completely forgotten them now. Why? Probably because they have proved irrelevant to our daily lives. Repetition must be relevant. It must also be enjoyable. Whereas a very young child will enjoy something being repeated again and again in *exactly* the same way, Juniors want variety. We need to have a single aim for our teaching on any one Sunday, and to use the time available in varied ways so that the one teaching point we are making is understood, learnt—and remembered. A tent pole needs several guy-lines to keep it firmly in position!

After some time has elapsed, we shall need to return again to what we taught, to see if it is still remembered, and to consolidate our teaching. This does not mean repeating exactly the same experience . . .

We shall not give a lesson on Joseph, for example, every few months, but we shall return again and again to some of the great themes of the Bible, illustrating them with different Biblical examples, and providing different activities for the children.

BUT DO THEY WANT TO KNOW?

Even when we provide all the means through which boys and girls can learn, they can still choose *not* to learn. The very young child will find sufficient satisfaction in just doing a particular thing, but as he grows older he will begin to want some other incentive or motivation—a feeling of achievement, the pleasure of seeing one's ideas and work accepted and appreciated, the approval of one's friends, and so on. Incentives do not have to be material rewards. (Those wanting to think more about prizes should read *Today's Children, Tomorrow's Church*.)

Very often, the incentive to learn which a child needs will lie in what *we* are. An old saying about a child, with a lot of truth in it, says: 'First I loved my teacher, then I came to love my teacher's Bible, and then I came to love my teacher's Lord.' What we are as people may make all the difference. *Do the children want to be like us*?

KNOW HOW TO PREPARE

There is no one way in which we should prepare. Some of us have the help of a preparation meeting; others do not. Here, however, are some basic principles to keep in mind.

1. Prepare early in the week. Difficult ideas to get across then have time to 'simmer' in the mind, and we may see something around us to help us illustrate a point.

2. When preparing, make sure you have enough time to pray before starting and after you have finished. Pray about your own understanding of what is to be taught, ask for a knowledge of the best methods to use and of each child, pray for the response to that particular teaching aim. Pray for others in the teaching team, too.

3. If you are using a guide or outline, be ready to adapt it to suit the needs of your own group. It gives *suggestions* and is not meant to be a strait-jacket. Do *not* lose sight of the aim, however.

4. Make the part you are going to play your own. Practise what you will say and how you will use any visual aid. Use your own words.

5. Make the briefest possible notes so that you do not have to take a detailed outline with you. You will then be more free to keep your eye on the children!

Chapter Six

CHILDREN, GOD AND THE BIBLE

Robert's behaviour that Sunday has been—for Robert—'normal'. For his Sunday School teacher, it had led her to describe him as 'a thorough nuisance'. Robert was one of those whose very presence means trouble. His teacher had sighed inwardly from the moment he walked through the door—and then she remembered some words of Jesus: 'Whoever receives one such child in My name receives Me'. If she received Robert with exasperation, she was receiving Christ that way. Impatience with Robert meant impatience with Him.

LIKE JESUS?

'I wonder what Jesus was really like when He was Robert's age?' she asked herself.

One thing we can be sure of: He who was perfect Man must also have been perfect Boy. Nevertheless, He was a *real* Boy—fully human—and must have developed normally in the way God planned originally for human growth and development.

So what do we think He was like as a perfect eight-year-old . . . ten-year-old . . . or whatever age the children we teach have reached? Delighting in new-found mastery over limbs, in new skills and abilities, how would He have shown His growing sense of independence? Is there a time when the child, his emotional development still incomplete, balancing on a wooden rail and crying out, 'Look at me!' is expressing *not* self-centred sinfulness but only the normal— *and right*—reaction of a growing child, enjoying what God has given him? Is there a time when the 'rough-and-tumble' is an expression *not* of sinfully aggressive instincts but of normal —and right—human development in a young child? When do we imagine the boy Jesus cried? Never? In what circumstances is it normal— *and right*—for a child to cry, simply because his emotions are those of

63

a child? Would Christ never have felt frustrated at being unable to do something just beyond His physical ability? Is a sense of frustration itself sinful—or is it how we *react* to that sense that can be marked by sin?

These are not easy questions to answer, and trying to answer them may raise other questions. Why not use this topic as a discussion-starter at a teachers' meeting?

At the age of seven, for example, Jesus must have had the body *and the emotions and mind* of a perfect seven-year-old. He must have had the human relationship with His heavenly Father that is appropriate to a perfect seven-year-old—and that is not the relationship that an adult has with the Father. It must have been a developing relationship. To deny this and want to regard the child Jesus as having the mental, emotional and spiritual maturity of an adult but the physical body of a child is to deny the reality of the Incarnation. He *did* become fully human . . . and what we want for a child at any particular age is that he or she should be as like the child Jesus as it is possible for a sinful human being to be.

It is true that Jesus had a special relationship with His Father because He was fully God, but He also had a perfect *human* relationship with Him because He was fully Man. If we say that no seven-year-old can have a real relationship with God, we are implying that Jesus, as a seven-year-old, cannot have had a human relationship with His Father either. Yet surely He loved and obeyed the Father God with the trust, love and understanding of a perfect seven-year-old? It is that same trust, love and understanding—though marred by being the response of an imperfect life—that we want to see in the lives of those we teach.

Children *can* have a real experience of God. Jesus put a child in the midst of His disciples (Matt. 18. 2) and went on to speak of such a child believing in Him (v. 5), or perishing (v. 14).

WHAT CAN CHILDREN UNDERSTAND?

Can they understand the Bible itself? There are some who say that very little in the Old Testament should be used with a child under thirteen years of age. Some will say that no Junior can have any grasp of what is meant by Jesus being a Saviour. Some would advise us not to teach seven-to-eleven-year-olds about the Holy Spirit. How are we to know what can and what can't be done, what should and what shouldn't be taught?

We have already looked at the need to understand something about the way a child develops and the limitations there are to his mental understanding at the pre-adolescent stage. This must not be forgotten—but nor must the fact that different children develop at different rates, and that some have a greater spiritual comprehension than others—even if they cannot put into words the things they have grasped. These are usually children with a rich background of Christian teaching, children from Christian homes. There are others, however, whose growth in spiritual understanding is not, humanly speaking, due to Christian parents, but to teachers. In either case, there has been the work of the Holy Spirit to give spiritual perception.

We need to make a distinction in our minds between these children and the boys and girls who have heard so much for so long that they are able to reproduce 'the right answers', and seem to have an understanding that is not really there. They can make all the 'right' responses and do so quite sincerely—but without really having made them their own. They are simply behaving in the way they think is expected of them—sometimes the result of Christian parents being over-anxious about the spiritual state of their children.

With this in mind, let us think what it is we need to teach and what a child is able to understand.

In the first place, we do not have to teach what *we think* about God. Our responsibility is to teach what God has revealed. The Bible is not just a record of how various people discovered truths about themselves, the world and God. It is God's authoritative word to us and records God's revelation of Himself as well as man's experience of Him. This is our source book, our authority—but that does not mean that we must tell only Bible stories, unexplained by any other story or teaching. Nor does it mean that the whole Bible is suitable for any and every age-group. We *shall* need to teach Biblical truth, but, as we have already seen, this needs to be illustrated with present-day 'parables', and taught in the way the child can best understand.

A child cannot think, for example, about abstract ideas like 'faith', 'obedience' or 'sin'. He *can* be told a story which shows someone whose faith leads him to obey (e.g., Abraham), or someone who commits specific sins (e.g., Achan). This he will understand if the teaching is made relevant—meaningful to him because it is related to his own awareness of times when he must trust or obey, or of times when he has done things he knew to be wrong.

In all our teaching, we must be asking ourselves, not only 'What basic *fact* am I trying to get across?' but also 'What is the appropriate *response* for a child to this fact?' Sometimes it will be possible to have an outward expression of this response—a prayer read aloud together, or an action in which the group can join. This might be the writing down individually of things the children want to confess to God, followed by a prayer and the burning of the pieces of paper. It might be a singing together of a chorus of praise. Movement is sometimes helpful, and children often appreciate the simple yet solemn 'ceremony' which they can devise and carry out together. They will often use a symbolism which they would find difficult to explain in words. This kind of activity will not be suitable for all groups, of course, and should always be the result of conviction on the teacher's or leader's part that it is what *God* wants in a particular situation. It will not be an 'everyday' occurrence, but something special.

READING THE BIBLE

The reading of a passage on which the teaching is to be based *before* the 'lesson' in which that teaching is given can create problems. If, for example, one had planned to introduce the story of Moses in the bulrushes in the way given on p. 53, without at first mentioning Moses at all, the whole approach would be spoilt by someone reading the story to the children before one began. In general, it is better if a Bible reading *supplements* the passage on which the 'lesson' is based or expresses a response to it—as might happen if verses from a psalm of worship were chosen to follow a lesson on the first two commandments.

The Bible reading does not have to be something taken by the leader to which the children listen passively. In fact, participation and variety are again important. Here are some ways in which the Bible can be used in the programme:

1. *Reading alternate verses.* The leader reads the first and every alternate verse; the children read the rest. It is important that each child has the same version—if not, write the passage on a sheet of paper. Alternatively, the children can be divided into two groups, reading alternately.

2. *Dramatized reading.* Individual children read the words of various

people who speak in the passage. Everyone else reads the rest. Choose good readers, prepared beforehand, for the solo parts—not easy in Bibles which do not use quotation marks.

3. *Deliberate mistakes.* The leader reads while children follow in their own Bibles. It is essential for all to have the same version. Children raise hands when a mistake is made. If this method is used *after* the teaching, the passage used in the 'lesson' can be read and children then listen *without* looking at their Bibles, so that the reading helps them to revise what they have learnt.

4. *Pause for the next word.* The leader reads while children follow in their own Bibles. When the leader pauses, the children read aloud the next word.

5. *Reading followed by quiz.* The leader first tells children to listen carefully as a quiz will follow, then reads the passage.

6. *Sword Drill.* This involves the reading of four separate verses, not consecutive. The children stand to attention and at the command 'Swords sheathed!' put their Bibles under their left arms. At 'Draw swords!' they take their Bibles in their right hands, hold them high, and say, "The sword of the Spirit, which is the word of God"— Ephesians 6. 17. The leader calls out a refreence. No child may begin to look for it until the word 'Charge!' The first to find it calls out the first word. It is usual to have about four references, each with one word (or idea) in common, so that the children can be listening for the common word, trying to discover what it is. If you call to the front the child who is first to find each verse, telling him to race for the next reference with the others but not to call out, you will end up with four children at the front. Let these compete to call out the common word after you have counted three. In the event of a draw, have an additional reference which the children can compete to find.

7. *Reading to encourage regular, personal Bible reading.* Occasionally, when specially wanting to encourage children to begin and persist in personal Bible reading, the day's *Quest* reading or the week's 'Bible Time' passage in *Adventurers* can be read. It is important to see that the *Quest* reading makes sense without the preceding and following days' passages. (The *Adventurers* passage is chosen to make sense on its own and supplements the teaching for the week in *Teaching Juniors.*) Precede the reading with a prayer in everyday language that we may understand what God wants us to know and do. (Psalm 119. 18 is commonly misunderstood by

children.) Follow this with the notes and questions, and then with a prayer arising out of the passage—as you would want the children to do on their own, so that they are shown *how* to have their own time of Bible reading and prayer at home.

'READING ROUND'?

Well what would *you* do? Let's look at what is happening.

It is fortunate that a fluent reader has the first verse of 1 Sam. 1. to read. Once he has read that, however, he may well lose interest, especially if the others do not read so well. He may become impatient with them and bored—and boredom will lead to trouble or to the child leaving.

The average reader will often count round and find the verse which will come to him—but he stops listening in order to look ahead at what he will need to read aloud, and so loses the sense of the whole passage.

When he does read his own verse, he may not read it with much personal understanding. *Until one has a mental age of ten years—*

and some children do not attain this until they are much older than ten—it takes all a child's concentration just to read the words aloud, and the meaning does not 'sink in' at the same time. After all, it is the practised adult eye that can take in a whole phrase at once and see the words which are coming while still reading aloud what precedes them. The child reads only one word at a time. This means that the child reading aloud may not even be taking in the meaning of what he is reading.

The poor reader, or the very shy child, may well leave if forced to read aloud. It *does* happen.

BIBLE 'WORK'

Bible 'work' is better than reading round. This means that the leader asks a question, gives a reference, and the children read the verse silently in order to find the answer to the question. A series of questions can cover several verses, e.g., 'God was going to tell His people something very important. How many days did they have to spend getting ready to hear about it (Exod. 19. 11)? What two things did they hear on the third morning (verse 16)? What two things did they see (verse 16)? What did they do (verse 18)? Why do you think they did that? Where did the people go and stand when Moses fetched them out of their tents (verse 17)? Where did Moses go (verse 20)?'

At the end of such a period of Bible work the children are likely to have not only *read* the passage, but *thought* about it. This is better than 'reading round' which should be left for much older groups.

POOR READERS OR NON-READERS

If we have many children with little reading ability, we must use teaching methods that cater for their needs. If we have only one poor reader, we must not bring *everything* down to that child's level or the others will become bored, and we must plan questions specially for the poor reader, and see that he or she is given plenty of encouragement and appreciated just as much as the others.

7–8 year-olds especially should not be expected, as a group, to be able to read and learn at the same time. Individual children with a reading ability far in advance of their actual age will be able to do so—but these are likely to be the exceptions in the group. Anyone teaching this age-group should look for a very simple—though still accurate—translation of the Bible. Today's English

Version will often be the answer, although sometimes the teacher may prefer to use his own simplified version of the RSV. He must take care, however, that the more basic vocabulary he chooses to use does not mean something different from the original.

Poor or non-readers cannot be expected to look up numerous verses from references, to read small print, or to understand long sentences. Choose one or two verses in a simple version. Write words on a large sheet of paper. Print letters but not in block capitals; poor readers will not recognize word-shapes. Read the words slowly, pointing to each in turn. The let children read aloud with you, as you repeat the words slowly, pointing to each in turn as you do so. Face the children; if necessary they will echo what you say. Even a non-reader can then 'read'—though a split second behind!—and will feel a sense of acceptance and achievement that will make him want to take part in the 'lesson' and learn.

MEMORIZING SCRIPTURE

'Junior' was learning his memory verse: 'For we are his workmanship, created in Christ Jesus for good works, which God prepared beforehand, that we should walk in them.'

An important verse for the Christian, yes . . . but even if David and Sue, Peter and Gillian are Christians, will they *understand* these words? They are fairly simple words for most Juniors—although 'workmanship' and 'beforehand' may convey very little. The sentence is very involved, however. What is more, the child is required to think about time in a very adult way if he is to understand this verse, and he simply hasn't a sufficiently developed sense of time.

He can *learn* the words, especially if the learning is made enjoyable—perhaps by writing the verse on a chalkboard, rubbing off words at random and asking the children still to read the verse, continuing this until the whole verse has been removed and children can repeat it all from memory. He can even *remember* the verse—for a long time if it is revised repeatedly, perhaps next week, and the week after, and then a month later, six months later, and so on. One day, many years in the future, he may recall the verse and start to think about it means . . . or it may become a verse which he knows and says so automatically that he does not think about it. Learning such a verse is not entirely without value . . . but could he not learn a verse which would be relevant and meaningful immediately, and help him in his life as a nine-year-old, a ten-year-old, and so on?

Children do not have to be taught *whole* verses if a part of a verse is more suitable. (The numbering of verses is not a part of Scripture as originally given, but something added much later.) Suitable verses (provided they are explained, of course) include: 'God has power to help' (2 Chron. 25. 8); 'The Lord is just in all his ways, and kind in all his doings' (Psa. 145. 17); 'Jesus . . . went about doing good' (Acts 10. 38); 'Christ died for our sins' (1 Cor. 15. 3); 'I am sorry for my sin' (Psa. 38. 18); 'I cannot see him, but he knows the way that I take' (Job 23. 9, 10) and 'To all who received him, who believed in his name, he gave power to become children of God' (John 1. 12).

Another way of teaching a memory verse is to represent each letter in the verse by a dash on a chalkboard. (Leave a space between words.) Divide the children into two teams. Each team in turn suggests a letter. (Choose a child who raises a hand rather than one who calls out.) If the letter chosen occurs in the text, write it in every place in which it occurs, and give that team the same number of points (e.g., if E is chosen and it occurs twice in the text, two points would be given). If the letter suggested does not occur at all, score a point for the 'quiz-master'. Children do not suggest *words*, even when they can see what an incomplete word, or even the whole text, is going to be. The knowledge will instead help them to choose the right letters. By the time the text is complete, it will also have been unconsciously memorized. If you wish, the reference can be included as well, and numbers suggested as well as letters.

BIBLE QUIZZES

A quiz is always popular with children, but it is best to produce your own questions, based on teaching that has been given to the children. Children will not think it very fair if the leader asks all sorts of difficult questions about unfamiliar stories and people. The general knowledge quiz that is not based on past teaching also puts the children from Christian homes at an advantage—and no child can help having the family into which he was born!

Quiz books can give helpful ideas, of course, about different kinds of quiz questions. There is, for example, the 'Who am I?' type of question. Three clues to the person's identity are prepared, and the children are given three points if they know the correct answer after hearing only the first clue, two points if they need two clues, and only one point if they need all three clues. If the person chosen was Peter, the clues might be:

1. I spoke to a great crowd and three thousand people believed and became Christians.
2. My brother was called Andrew.
3. Once I said three times that I didn't even know Jesus.

Questioning is itself an art—but one which we can learn. It is dealt with in Chapter 8—but remember that it applies as much to leading a quiz as to asking questions in the course of our teaching.

There are various ways of scoring points in a quiz. One which children greatly enjoy is based on the game of Noughts and Crosses. For this, two teams are needed. As each team scores, let the child answering correctly decide where to put a nought or a cross (depending on which team he is in). If an answer is incorrect, do not pass the question to the opposing team; in this method of scoring that often gives a clear advantage to the other team.

Other methods of scoring can often be devised by adapting ideas used on radio or television quiz programmes or in children's games (e.g., Snakes and Ladders), or by using charts which depict competing figures (e.g., knights climbing a castle tower to rescue a girl at the top, rockets racing through the sky, small toy cars moving round a track).

Chapter Seven

LET'S BE FLEXIBLE

Supposing one had the opportunity of planning a whole hour of teaching/learning and worship for Juniors, how might one go about it? Some may be in situations where no one has thought of changing anything for very many years, or where such a change is not approved of. We suggest that you still read this chapter; there is no knowing when you may have the opportunity of introducing new ideas!

Let's look at one 'Sunday School' group in action.

It was about 11.15 a.m., and as the last people moved away from the church after the Morning Service, the boys and girls came streaming in. Their younger brothers and sisters had been left at the church halls for their own activities, and those of secondary school age met at a totally different time. The children coming into the church were the Juniors; 'Explorers', as their group was called, was about to start.

As they came in, laughing and chattering, music was coming softly from a tape-recorder—a Christian folk group. The children divided into their two teams and went to 'sign on' at their own team chart—put ready, with a pencil beside it, in its usual place, for this was the regular method of recording attendance and one that made the children feel more 'grown-up' and that did not intrude into teaching time later on.

They then went to their own class-group's area of the room where their leader was ready with some practical work for them to begin on as soon as they arrived. This was a large enough Explorer group to have four 'classes' within it, one for each of the year-groups. Today, models were being made by the first years (those who would be having their eight birthday some time between the beginning of September when they moved into the Junior section of their day school and the end of August in the year following). Using polystyrene ceiling tiles as a base and pipe-cleaner figures, they were turning their thoughts back to the previous week's teaching on the way God cared for Elijah and provided him with the food he needed. They were themselves revising what they had learnt, and were also telling the story to absentees who had missed it. As their leader moved among them, she was able to ask questions about the models, the story, and what it teaches us today—all in a very informal way, among the conversation about John's birthday party the previous day, Sarah's new shoes, the music exam that Jane would be taking during the week, and David's cat which had had kittens. The whole activity had been planned to take the first fifteen minutes.

Mr. Stewart had decided that his second-years should concentrate on the basic spiritual truth taught the previous week, and make a frieze on the extent of God's care for us, which they could display to the other boys and girls later in the programme. They were illustrating the phrase, 'God cares about . . .', with incidents from a child's everyday life at home, at school, at play with other children, in visiting relatives, going to the dentist, and so on. Each child was drawing and colouring a picture for the frieze and preparing a sentence to say about it: 'God cares when we....................................
.............................and He knows that....................and can........................ '

Meanwhile the third-year group was at work on a visual aid which their leader would use with all the children later in the session. For the first page of a 'flip-over' chart, the children were looking in magazines and newspapers for pictures that might at first make some people think God does *not* care about what goes on in this world—pictures of unrest, anger, violence, unhappiness, natural disasters, etc. Another child, with a felt-tipped pen, was inking over the leader's pencilled outlines for the second sheet of the chart—the words 'God *does* care'—and another was doing the same for the third sheet—'Then why do these things happen?' Two children were finding and cutting out pictures of a present-day boy and girl to paste on to a square of thin card that could be slipped into two vertical slots on the last sheet of the visual aid. Again the leader was able to listen to the children and chat with them as the work was done.

The fourth-year group were being 'stretched' mentally—given something to work at with the incentive of gaining a further gold star on a chart that recorded the special projects given only to these

10 and 11 year-old boys and girls, who had extra privileges and extra responsibilities in their final year before joining the Bible Class. This week, they were working in pairs on assignment cards involving some very simple Bible study. Each 'Let's find out' card gave the reference for a short passage about someone whose story had been the subject of the teaching at some time during the previous year or two. The boys and girls had to read the passage and complete the card, which read: 'God cared about............................ when............................ He............................' There were additional cards for those who completed their first with plenty of time to spare.

The music on the tape-recorder had been quietly faded out at the beginning of this fifteen minutes of activity, but five minutes before it was due to end, the tape-recorder was switched on again, and while the music played very softly, the children were told that they had only five more minutes. Each group-leader then saw to it that children finished the particular task they were doing and did not start anything else. Scissors and pencils were put into each group's box of equipment and rubbish was cleared away into a waste-paper tin. At the very end of the activity time, the volume of the tape-recorder was turned up as a sign that everything must now be put down and children seated facing the front by the time the music had again been turned down in volume until it faded out. As the music became quieter, so did the children—for this was a familiar signal to them. The first years' models had been placed on the table at the front not only to keep them from being played with or from being a distraction, but so that public recognition might be given to what they had achieved. Any absentees of the previous week could be told about Elijah's experience of God's care as some of the models were held up by the first-years' group leader and shown to the entire age-range.

After this, the children sang 'God, who made the earth', reminding themselves of the extent of God's care. During this, four of the 10–11 year-olds took round the offering bags (made by themselves earlier in the year) and received the children's offering. As this was given to a particular project overseas in which the children are taking a practical interest, they were reminded that this is one way in which they could show *their* care, and the people to whom it was to be given were prayed for.

The frieze was then displayed by Mr. Stewart, who took over at that point from Mr. Maxwell (the over-all leader), and this was followed by a prayer led by volunteers from the children who suggested one-sentence 'Thank You' prayers related to God's care.

Miss Green was now ready at the front with the visual aid her group had helped to make, and for the next ten minutes she taught the entire group.

After this, she took her guitar and taught the children a negro spiritual that expresses the spiritual truth behind this whole programme—'He's got the whole wide world in His hands.' Of course, she explained that God has no hands and why this is so, and asked the children what they thought the song meant.

Mr. Maxwell had been checking on the fourth-years' assignment cards in the last few minutes and now called out the children to read aloud what they had discovered, first telling the whole group that there would be a 'Who am I? 'quiz on these people in the Bible after the cards had been read out. The quiz gave an opportunity for team points to be awarded, but it was more important than that. It continued the teaching and used yet another means of helping children to absorb the first part of the aim underlying the whole programme: the God who cares about us is a God who allows us to choose whether or not we care about Him.

After the quiz, there was a chorus, 'All that I am He made me', with its reminder that apart from the Lord Jesus Christ we cannot be the people we hope to be.

The children then divided again into their class-groups for the remainder of the teaching (Elijah on Mount Carmel and the need to choose where our allegiance is to be—not, of course, expressed in those words to children). This took a further fifteen minutes. It was followed by a final five minutes with the total group gathered together again for the reading of Joshua's words to his people in Josh. 24. 14, 15, the chorus 'Choose you this day' and a prayer that each might come to make the right choices as they were presented, especially when faced with the choice of obeying or not obeying Christ's call to follow Him.

SUPPOSE WE HAVEN'T AN HOUR?

This is clearly not the kind of programme that can be planned in detail for those with less than an hour available, but as we look at the principles underlying it, we shall begin to see what is its value and how it can be adapted.

In the hour's programme described, every item is an integral part of the whole and has a particular contribution to make towards the achieving of the aim. This is very different from the more traditional programme which could be shown this way, with the shaded part representing worship.

TRADITIONAL PROGRAMME FOR ONE HOUR

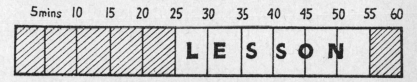

If the average adult church service were shown by such a sketch, the pattern would be identical, with a sermon in place of the lesson. This is, however, a pattern which assumes that the people taking part, whether adults or children, are ready and able to worship from the moment the hour begins. But do most of our Sunday School children have the spiritual experience to be so ready to enter into worship in a sincere and meaningful way? What is more, does the very fact that they *are* children, and neither physically nor emotionally nor socially nor mentally mature, mean that a different kind of activity is needed first? This needs to be something which will form a natural bridge for the child who has come from a non-Christian background and which will prepare him for the teaching which is to follow. Teaching in its turn—if good—should give rise to worship. If a child is first able to learn something more about God the worship which follows can indeed be a real response and not merely an outward act.

A NEW APPROACH (*see diagram overleaf*)

If we draw a plan for the programme described at the beginning of this chapter, we shall find that activity comes first, with teaching and worship interspersed as one item leads naturally on to the next.

Where is the 'lesson'? It is not *just* the group-time; part of it comes in the teaching given to all the Juniors when the visual aid is used. The 'lesson' has in this case been split, and only a part of

5	10	15	20	25	30	35	40	45	50	55	60
ACTIVITY IN	CLASS-GROUPS		HYMN·OFFERING·PRAYER	TEACHING WITH VISUAL AID		SINGING	REPORT FROM ASSIGNMENT CARDS AND QUIZ	SINGING	GROUP-TIME	FURTHER TEACHING	READINGS·CHORUS·PRAYER

it given in groups. *We have to bear in mind that learning is not restricted to a time called 'the lesson'; it can go on throughout the hour.*

With this approach, we cease cutting the time in two and calling it 'the first half-hour' (worse still, 'the preliminaries') and 'the lesson'. *Teaching and worship are integrated into a total-hour programme, all centred on the aim for the day.* We stop having a 'hymn-and-a-thing' sandwich—an assortment of items separated from one another by a hymn (or a chorus), and often unrelated to one another.

A good programme will be marked by the same features as a good 'lesson'—interest, variety, relevance, plenty of opportunities for children to take an active part, and each part leading on from the one before and leading up to whatever is to follow.

THE PROBLEM IS . . .

'We couldn't possibly do that. We have to have all the 3's to 15's meeting together for the first half and then split into smaller groups—all in the same room—for the lesson.'

You certainly have a problem—and the children know it, too, for no one can produce a programme that is really geared to every age-group all the time. To switch from an item to suit the under-fives to one for the teenagers, to another for the Juniors, and so on, is a very poor second-best, only to be allowed if there is *really* no alternative. Is there no other room—no kitchen or church vestry perhaps—that could be used? Is there no home that could be used? Could some of the children meet at a different time from the others? Be careful, however, not to have a different time for the under-eights from that for the slightly older brothers and sisters who bring them.

AND ANOTHER PROBLEM . . .

'Our Sunday School really only meets for the second half of the Morning Service. We join in the first half of the church service and then go off on our own.'

There are advantages and disadvantages to this—and the leader of such a group is recommended to read *Today's Children, Tomorrow's Church*, where the need to compensate for the disadvantages (e.g., with a week-night club) is discussed. One of the practical problems is that there is little time for much more than the lesson itself once the children have left the adult service. This is where it is worth asking oneself, 'What have the children already had in the service?' They may have sung several hymns, in which case we can have some other item before the 'lesson' and end with a chorus or short hymn related to our teaching. If we have thirty-five minutes we might plan a five-minute introductory item, twenty-five minutes for teaching (including the use of acting or work-sheets,etc. —see chapter 7) and five minutes for a hymn and a prayer, or for learning a memory verse and for prayer. The introductory item might be a quiz, or the compiling over several weeks of a frieze or of a group zig-zag book from pictures drawn at home by the children during the previous week, or the making of a visual aid to be used in the 'lesson', etc. Whatever this first item is, it needs to be in contrast to what has preceded it in the church service itself.

TEAM COMPETITION

One of the things that can help the organization and carrying out of Sunday's programme, however long or short it may be, is the use of teams. In this way, we can harness and use a child's competitive spirit so that instead of it being used solely to further his *own* interests, he is encouraged to co-operate with others in a team and work for the good of them all. Team points can be awarded for attendance, bringing a Bible, bringing a new member, giving correct answers in a quiz, remembering the previous week's memory verse, etc. The points are recorded by the *child's* name, but given to the *team*.

A chart which shows the progress of each team will help to keep up interest, but no chart should be used for more than two months, or the team trailing along at the bottom will become discouraged and may stop trying. It can be a good idea to change the membership and the names of the teams if they are too uneven in achievement. Try to keep friends together in the same team if at all possible; children could write down the names of those they would most like to be with and give these to you for sorting out into teams. Make sure they understand, however, that try as you may it will not be possible for *everyone* to be with *every* boy or girl that he or she has listed.

In working out the teams it also helps if you avoid having all the younger children in one group and all the older ones in another. Try, too, to have the same number of boys in each team. Do not have two separate teams of boys and girls; competition between the sexes is not really a good thing as God made us to work with the opposite sex, not to compete against one another. Such a spirit will only make it more difficult for Junior boys and girls to accept one another as equally human!

It often helps to be able to identify the team of any particular boy or girl. This can be achieved by having children seated in teams rather than in class-groups for much of the programme—but there are disadvantages here for the leader of a class-group wanting to be with his or her own group. Another means of identification is to issue badges of different colours for the different teams. Children may forget to wear these, however, or may lose them—unless you decide to distribute them to children as they arrive each week and to collect them at the end of the session.

SOME IDEAS FOR TEAM CHARTS
Children will often have good ideas to contribute—frequently topical, e.g., a space-craft for each team on a race to the moon; an Olympic athlete for each team, etc. An idea may come to one as a result of seeing a picture in a newspaper colour supplement. An example of this is a map of ancient wrecks in the coastal waters around Britain that gave rise to a round-Britain treasure race to collect 'buried treasure'. Ladders can be made from string laced through fairly stiff card with a pipe-cleaner figure to climb each team's ladder. The gradual descent of divers to the ocean bed can be recorded by increasing the number of 'bubbles' (linen ring reinforcements produced for loose-leaf folders). Balloonists in their craft—a different colour for each team—can be hoisted up the wall of your hall until one reaches the ceiling. Racing cars can move round a circuit, missionaries go on their journeys to other lands, ancient explorers discover new countries, etc. Team charts

do not always need to be two-dimensional sheets of card. Pipe-cleaner men can move round a 'maze' drawn with a felt-tipped pen on a polystyrene ceiling tile.

Why not have a visual reminder of which team won the last competition? One way of doing this is to cut a shield from hardboard or polystyrene and drape round it a ribbon or braid in the colour of the winning team. Change the colour of the ribbon when a different team wins a competition.

Teams can also be given responsibility, so that each team takes it in turn to take responsibility for moving chairs if this is necessary, tidying up after the session, giving out and collecting materials, etc. If you have a large number in each team, these tasks could be seen as the special responsibilities of the 10–11 year-olds who should be encouraged to take jobs of this kind and given privileges, too, that the others do not have. One of these older children could be asked to make out a list of who is to take the offering each week, for example, and to write out the list and decorate it so that it can be displayed. In little ways like this, children will be helped to see the group as *theirs*, not just as something run by adults *for* them.

From time to time, part of the week's programme could be prepared and presented by teams taking this in rotation. Each team should be given the help of a leader. Children can lead in prayer, ask quiz questions, announce hymns and choruses, etc. Junior boys and girls are often used to doing this at school and prove more capable than many of us would have thought. We should give them the opportunity to play this active part in the programme—with adequate preparation and help, of course. Other children will often respond more readily to those of their own age.

It must still be remembered, however, that up-dating methods and including child-participation is no substitute for prayerful teachers who really know their Lord and care about the children.

Chapter Eight

LEARNING THROUGH DOING

'I hear and I forget; I see and I remember; I do and I understand.'
This saying is true for us all. Have you ever had to learn how to use
an intricate piece of equipment? An instruction book helps if it
has diagrams, but the easiest way to learn something new is to
watch someone else do it—and then do it oneself, one step at a time.

How many times have you written down something in order to
help you remember it? Even if you lost the note or list and had no
visual reminder after all, the very act of writing it down helped you
to remember.

A LESSON FOR JUNIORS

Let us look now at a 'lesson' for Junior boys and girls and see how
they are helped to learn through doing.

The story of Christ stilling the storm is being used to teach that
there is nothing we need fear if we know that Jesus is with us and
have faith in Him. There is an introduction, a development, and a
conclusion which takes the form of prayer. The application is not
in a 'final few words'—but throughout.

The introduction starts with something in the children's experience.
They are asked to write down anything which boys or girls of their
age sometimes feel afraid of. Gummed labels are used for this (one
for each item), and they are stuck in a vertical column just right of
centre of the group leader's chart—a large sheet of paper with
nothing else on it at present. Children can do the writing individually
or in pairs.

The 'bridge' to the Bible story is built by the leader asking,
'Were Jesus' disciples ever afraid of anything? When?' If the storm
on the lake is mentioned, further questions follow to draw the
story from the children. If it is clear that the children do not already
know the story, it is told to them. Younger Juniors, while listening
to the story, are encouraged to act what they think the disciples

would have been doing. Whether the children know the story or not, they are encouraged to use their imagination and decide what would have been happening between 'the boat was already filling' (Mark 4. 37) and 'But he was asleep . . . and they woke him') v. 38. (No mention is made in the account of the disciples trying to get the boat under control, bale out water—or do anything at all. As children imagine all this, possibly acting it as well, they will get some sense of the fear and panic that was felt.)

When the facts of the story have been established, the leader begins to provoke further though about them by asking the children *why* they think Jesus said 'Why are you afraid?' By answering questions, the children are helped to think about who Christ is, what difference His presence in the boat might have made, why the disciples failed to have faith in Him, etc. They are then asked two very important questions: 'What did the disciples learn about Jesus?' (the answers to this are written on the left-hand side of the leader's chart), and 'What did they learn about themselves?' (answered orally but not written down).

Children again work individually or in pairs, each taking one of the fears previously written on a label for the chart and writing an imaginary note to help a boy or girl with that fear. With younger Juniors, this might be done orally with the leader writing down what the children suggest. This gives the leader an opportunity to discover to what extent the children are already able to relate the Bible story to the present-day needs of children.

The memory verse is then introduced and learnt: Jesus said, 'My peace I give to you . . . let not your hearts be troubled, neither let them be afraid' (John 14. 27). The leader explains what 'peace' means in this context. (Children may think of it only as a state of no physical fighting or war.) To the tips of the fingers of his left hand he attaches small self-stick labels to spell out the word P-E-A-C-E, holding his hand with the palm facing the children. He asks, 'What did the disciples need if they were to have peace inside even with a storm raging?' To the right-hand finger-tips he attaches labels to spell F-A-I-T-H, and explains this. (The identification of these two words with the ten fingers is an aid to memory.) A pair of hands is shown on the work-page provided in *Adventurers*, and children are given this so that they may label the finger-tips. They then write down (with or without help) their conclusion to two sentences: 'Faith' means .... 'Peace' means ....

To conclude, the leader asks the children what could be put into a prayer about all that they have been learning. He either takes their suggestions and leads them in prayer himself, or has volunteers to lead the children in one or two-sentence prayers.

PARTICIPATION

Which of these ways of participating in a lesson are used in the preceding examples?

1. Simple discussion prompted by questions to be answered.
2. Questions based on a Bible verse or passage.
3. Simple actions to help children imagine themselves in a Biblical situation.
4. Miming a Bible story.
5. Reading a prepared script involving 'role-play'—identifying oneself with someone else, so as to realize more about the implications of the story.
6. Children themselves helping to tell a well-known Bible story.
7. Quiz questions to test children's memory of a story they can be expected to know.
8. Helping to make or use the visual aid (chart or model).
9. Writing or drawing on a work-sheet (such as *Adventurers*) or in a note-book.
10. Making up their own playlet to illustrate the lesson aim.

ALL CHILDREN ARE TALKERS

Few would want to argue with that—though some children may be too shy to talk freely in front of others. Even the shyest of us, however, can talk about something exciting we have seen or experienced, provided we have a sympathetic listener whom we know well. Our problem may not be with the shy, of course—but with the over-talkative. Do we really want to encourage boys and girls to talk?

It has been said that children remember 10% of what they hear, 50% of what they see, 60% of what they say, and 90% of what they do. Whether those figures are accurate or not and for how long children remember, the fact remains that something a child has to put into his own words is learnt and remembered more effectively than something that is merely said *to* him—or even *shown* to him visually.

Questioning

The principal way in which we shall want children to make a spoken contribution is in the answering of questions. Questioning enables us to find out three basic things:
1. Were the children even listening?
2. Did they understand?
3. Have they accepted what I said as true and made the appropriate response?

Questioning was a teaching method used by Christ. He questioned, for example, the lawyer to whom He told the story of the Good Samaritan (Luke 10. 36), the Pharisees (Matt. 22. 41-45), Phillip when faced with the problem of five thousand hungry people (John 6. 5), the people in the Temple (Matt. 21. 23-31, 40).

Questions and answers form such a natural part of our everyday speech that we may think there is nothing we need to learn about questioning. Nevertheless, it is an art—but one that can be learnt. Silence instead of an answer from the children may not mean that they are stupid; it may be that the question put to them was not a good one. But what makes a question 'good'?

Questions must be clear—not ambiguous. 'Where did Jesus come from?' is an ambiguous question; there is more than one possible—and correct—answer. 'Bethlehem'; 'God'; 'heaven'—these are only three of the possible answers. If the questioner had wanted the answer 'Bethlehem', a better question would have been 'In which town was Jesus born?'

Questions should not have only a 'Yes' or 'No' answer. 'Did Joseph and Mary find Jesus in the temple?' can be answered without much thought—and if the first quick answer is wrong, the second is bound to be right. Here, a better question would have been 'Where did Joseph and Mary find Jesus?'

Questions can ask who, when, where, what, why or how? Questions that begin with one of these words demand more thought, especially if they are about actions and truths as well as people, places and things. 'Where did Joseph and Mary find Jesus?' could be followed by 'What was He doing there? Why? How did Mary and Joseph feel about it? Why was Jesus surprised that they had not known where He was? Whom did He mean by "My Father"?'

Questions can probe behind the facts. Such a question would be 'Why do you think Mary and Joseph had not looked first in the Temple? What do you think Mary and Joseph thought about their son? What makes you think that? Do you think it would always have been easy for Jesus to obey His earthly parents?'

Questions should always provoke thought. You may have noticed that every one of the questions in the previous paragraph included the word 'think'. These are not questions that can be answered superficially with an obvious 'right' answer. We should make it clear to children that we want to know what *they* think; we do not have one particular answer all ready in our minds—an answer which we are wanting them to give. Some children are very good at using a stock of glib answers, such as 'Pray', 'God', or 'Jesus'.

If we suspect that a particular child's answer to a question, though correct, was largely an almost automatic response, we can always ask another question before giving any indication as to whether the answer was in fact the right one: 'I see, Janet—but what makes you think that?'

Questions should ask only one thing at a time. A multiple question is confusing: 'Was Jesus only asking questions in the temple or was He answering them as well?' The children may answer 'Yes', but as the answer to one of the questions asked is 'Yes' but to the other is 'No', how does one know which question the child is answering? We ourselves are now in some confusion—but some children will have been so confused by two questions having been asked at once that they may answer neither.

Questions need to be prepared. Few of us will be able to ask good questions on the spur of the moment. What is more, we may well have a wide range of ability in the class and want to plan questions that will suit particular children. Karen is not very bright. She cannot read yet and easily feels discouraged. Her teacher, Mr. Stewart, must not draw attention to her by singling her out with a specially easy question so he will not say, 'Now, Karen, this question is for you.' Instead, he will ask the question, let all the children put up their hands, and look around the group before saying, 'Karen?' Mr. Stewart will not forget Paul either, for Paul has grown up in a Christian home and 'knows everything'. There will be a specially difficult question prepared with Paul in mind!

Children should be allowed to ask questions. 'Does anyone want to ask a question?' A question *asked* by a child often reveals more to us than a question *answered* by a child. We must make sure that we go at the pace of the children—not at our own speed. Some groups also like to have a 'question box' kept in one corner of the room with writing materials beside it. Children can post questions to any leader, who replies in writing—sometimes suggesting that the two get together to talk about the answer. No question should be allowed to remain in the box for week after week unanswered; make sure the box is emptied at the end of the session and that replies are ready for the children at the beginning of the following week's meeting.

What about wrong answers from children? Let us first make sure that it really *is* a wrong answer. Sometimes children come out with a statement we certainly did not expect, but which—when the child is encouraged to explain further—turns out to be a valuable contribution. Such an answer sometimes casts new light on a familiar Bible story for everyone —including the teacher.

If it *is* a wrong answer, let us be as encouraging as possible—but not dishonest! 'Well tried—but you're not quite right yet. Can anyone else help?' may be a way to do this.

Children as story-tellers

The Bible story is, of course, not the whole of a lesson and we do not tell it merely so that children should know the facts of the story. We include it because it is the God-given vehicle for conveying a particular spiritual truth. We shall choose a story that conveys clearly to a child the truth we want him to see, and which does it without bringing the child face to face with concepts he is too young to be able to grasp, or leading him to dangerous misunderstandings. Because we shall not be using the whole Bible with Juniors, we shall often find ourselves wanting to refer to an incident that the children learned about while in the Primary department. We may find that the story we are using is familiar because it has been told at school— even 'We had this at school *this week!*'

There are dangers in assuming that the facts *are* already known, so that we can go straight on to the implications and what the story means for us today. The children may have heard either a dramatized version which added to the facts, or a biased version given by an unbelieving adult who could not accept the story as it is but gave his or her own interpretation of it. We need to find out *what* the children know when they say 'We know this one.'

Often better-known stories can be presented so that the group-leader encourages his 'class' or group to help him tell the story. He can add to the parts he wants to stress and direct the children to an unknown part by reading particular verses with them. Another way to do this and hold the attention and interest of the whole group is to let one child tell the story while the others listen for mistakes or omissions. If they think they detect either, they can 'challenge' by raising a hand, but must then say what was wrong and what the correct version should have been. If right, the challenger is given a team point; if wrong, the point goes to the story-teller.

Children's own experience
A further way in which children can play a verbal part is by contributing from their own experience—e.g., sharing together times when they felt worried about something will help to bring home the relevance of a lesson on trusting God about what happens. This does not necessarily mean saying 'Tell me about a time when you felt worried.' It is sometimes better to make a question sound impersonal: 'Let's think of times when boys and girls might feel worried.' Often, a child will want to make a contribution, perhaps at a time when we had not planned for this, because an experience he has had has suddenly come to mind. What to us seems an interruption may be very significant in helping the child to apply the teaching to himself.

CHILDREN AND WORK-SHEETS
Opposite is what happens when the application is left to the end and given in a solid 'dose'. Like the pill left whole in the jam, which the child may be able to find with his tongue and spit out when his mother turns her back, the teaching that is not made an integral part of the story and other activities and woven throughout the whole of the teaching can be easily rejected.

One way in which the teaching can be most effectively applied—and applied to each individual child—is through a work-sheet . . . something which needs to be written or drawn. This might involve drawing oneself in a particular situation. Sometimes the children could be asked to complete a prayer which makes the teaching personal or write, draw or answer questions about what a fictitious child should do in a given situation (testing the child's understanding of what we have been trying to put across).

Other purposes for which a work-sheet can be used include:

Revision—e.g., numbering pictures in the correct order so that they tell the story; writing titles for pictures to summarize the story;

deciding whether statements telling the story are true or false; answering crossword or other puzzles to revise the story.

Finding out—e.g., questions with references to look up; Bible verses to decipher and then learn; questions with the answers given as jumbled words.

Identification with a Bible character—e.g., completing an imaginary letter, diary or newspaper item as though personally involved or an eye-witness; imagining (or looking up in the Bible) someone's thoughts and words and adding them to a picture.

FACING THE PROBLEM

No. 1—'We've no tables.'

Get some stackable tables if you can . . . if there's storage space . . . and space to erect them! If you have to meet in a church building with fixed pews, do not give up all thought of children writing, drawing, making models and friezes, and so on. Children have been known to produce a frieze down the length of the aisle, and work on pulpit steps, the flat top of an organ, or the pews. A simple and effective solution to the problem is to make enough boards, approx. 12″ x 9″, for each child to have one. Hardboard will last better than thick cardboard, but for short-term use, such as a week's Holiday Club, the strongest cartons discarded by the grocer can be cut into pieces and put to use.

No. 2—'The children don't want to write anything.'

This is not a general reaction, but may be the attitude of some whose human nature says, 'Sit back and take it easy—you don't want to do this; it's too much like hard work.' This can be said about thinking—or singing—or praying—or reading the Bible . . . if the child chooses to react that way. Some children *are* more lazy than others—but if we want what is best for the child, we shall not give in to persistent statements of an 'I can't be bothered' nature, but adopt an attitude of good-humoured, firm insistence. Have a look at the windows, however. Are you sure that the children are not dozy because of inadequate ventilation?

Sometimes it is sufficient to have a pack of fine-tipped, coloured felt pens for children to use instead of ordinary pencils.

No. 3—'They're no good at writing and drawing and they know it.'

Are you expecting too much of them? Appreciation of what they do manage to produce, and plenty of encouragement, will achieve a lot more than criticism.

No. 4.—'There's one child who's terribly slow—he'd never finish.'

Do not wait for the slowest child, or the fast ones, rapidly getting bored, will cause trouble. Assure the slower ones that it does not matter if they have not finished yet, and tell all the children to put down their pencils and look at you. If the work-sheets are likely to provide distraction because there is something else on them that children want to read, insist that the sheets are put down, and the boards—if these are being used—are put on top of them. (And having given a firm, definite order, insist on being obeyed and do not pretend that you have not noticed a child who disobeys; he will probably be aware of the fact that you *have* noticed—and done nothing!)

Chapter Nine

MAKING IT LIVE

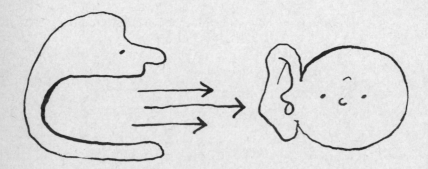

No—teaching others is *not* like this, the teacher all mouth and no ears, while the hearer is all ears and no mouth! Nevertheless, the teacher does need to do *some* talking—stating, explaining, illustrating from everyday examples and from the Bible. Let's think more now about how to do these things.

JESUS THE TEACHER

No one taught as He did—with power and authority, in a way that made great crowds hear Him gladly (Mark 12. 37), and taking the simple, everyday things of life to illustrate spiritual truth. He spoke of seed-sowing and harvest, supper-parties and wedding feasts, coins, sheep, lamp-stands, carrying soldiers' packs for the army of occupation, wild flowers and birds, pearls and pigs, grapes and thistles. He used stories—a runaway son, an absentee landlord, a good Samaritan. He lit up the truth.

What everyday sights, sounds and recurrences might He have used if He had been teaching in *our* home-town—today? Look around at the area in which the children live, look at the things you handle day by day, think of what interests the children and start to collect illustrations. It is much easier to write down an illustration of a Biblical truth when you notice it than to have to think of one when you need it, so a notebook can be very useful. If you have a loose-leaf book, you can arrange the items according to subject—faith, obedience, sin, etc. Children cannot think in abstract terms as adults can —and even some adults find it very hard to understand 'faith', for instance, without an everyday illustration.

EXPLAINING SPIRITUAL TRUTH

Here is an example of how something within most children's own experience can be used to help reach a spiritual truth.

Jane has spots—but the doctor says that there is something more deeply wrong than the red blotches on her skin. She has measles. The spots are only a part of the trouble, the part that shows on the outside. She has spots only because she has measles. It is what is wrong inside that is really the trouble. It is just the same with us. It is what is wrong *inside* us that is really the trouble. What shows on the outside—bad temper, selfish behaviour, unkind words, and things like that—is there because we *are* wrong. Deep down in the real ME is something that is turned away from God, spoilt by Satan, showing itself in the wrong things we think and say and do. It is what the Bible calls 'sin'. When we want to please ourselves, make excuses, lie, cheat, steal, disobey, answer back, show off, think wrong thoughts, or do anything like that, it is because we are sinful people. We sin *because* we are sinful. Our sins show what we are really like—not on the outside, but in the way God sees us.

ILLUSTRATIONS THAT MISLEAD

A boy was once sitting listening to a preacher talking about sin. He described it as being like a blot in a spotless white book, so spoiling it that the book had to be rejected.

'But sir,' the boy objected, 'that's not fair.'

He was, of course, quite right. It was the illustration that was wrong—for sin in a human life is *not* like one blot in an otherwise perfect book. It is more like a cloth that has fallen into a pot of paint and is stained in every part. Every area of man's life is stained and spoilt by sin.

The illustration here was misleading, because it gave a wrong picture. It is important to ask oneself if a particular word or story *could* conjure up a wrong mental picture in the mind of the literalistic Junior with a fairly limited vocabulary. 'The flight into Egypt' can lead to a child thinking of air travel; 'escape' would be a better word.

USING CHILDREN'S EXPERIENCE

Whenever a completely new word needs to be introduced, it must be explained—preferably likening it to something already within a child's experience. For example, in the everyday world of the children you know, what is the nearest thing to the bitumen used as mortar in building the Tower of Babel (Gen. 11. 3) and as a sealing agent for the woven basket made for Moses (Exod. 2. 3)?

Sometimes a story can convey a spiritual truth—provide a modern parable—by being set in the life of a child today:

'Two children were blowing up balloons for a party. Peter took the first one—a red one—and began. Slowly the ballon began to swell—the size of an apple, the size of a grapefruit, the size of a melon . . . "Go on", said Philip. "You can get it as big as a football." Peter looked doubtful. "Do you really think so?" he asked. "Yes, of course," answered Philip. "Well, go on—you carry on," said Peter, handing over both balloon and pump. "Well—perhaps it *is* big enough after all," said Philip.

'Philip thought he believed that the balloon could be blown up to be as big as a football—until he was asked to do something to *show* he believed it. Then he discovered that he was not sure.

'We can "believe *about*" something, but not really *trust*. Philip believed something *about* the balloon—that it would stretch to an even bigger size—but he did not really *trust* the balloon not to burst right in front of him. In other words, he could not *act* on what he believed . . . .

'You might *believe* that a boy at school would be a good leader and yet—perhaps very wisely—not trust yourself to him to the point of saying you'll do whatever he wants. Putting our trust in the Lord Jesus is more than just believing certain things about Him; it means giving ourselves completely to Him and being ready to do whatever He wants.'*

---

* From *Teaching Juniors*, SU's quarterly magazine for use with Junior Sunday Schools and similar groups.

STORY-TELLING

We shall often find ourselves called upon to tell a story. Usually it will be a Biblical incident, told in the Bible in very few words. To make it 'come alive' for children, we shall need to tell it in an expanded form, in our own words.

Some people *are* better story-tellers than others—but everyone can improve, given help and practice. Here is the help; the practice is up to you!

The background work—preparing the story

1. *Get inside the story.*

Imagine it all as though it had happened to you. Think how you would have felt; picture what you would have seen; 'listen' for the sounds you would have heard. There is room for you to use your imagination here; you will not be contradicting the Biblical narrative.

In the example that follows, the writer has thought very hard about the sounds, because they are so important to the story:

'Gideon explained his plan. Quietly they crept to their positions—all round the Midianite camp. It was dark and very quiet—just the sounds of camels grunting and then a tent flapping.

'Then Gideon's trumpet call rang out, followed by the rest, echoing all through the valley—sounding like thousands and thousands. At the same time the jars were broken and the torches waved in the darkness. They were *all around* the camp! The night was filled with shouting: "The sword of the Lord and of Gideon!" That, too, rang out *all around* the camp.

'There was absolute pandemonium—camels lurching into each other and into tents, and men rushing about, striking at each other. No one knew what was happening, and soon the whole camp was fleeing in all directions.'

2. *Remember your aim.*

Which part of the story is of greatest importance in achieving your aim? You will need to emphasize this part and possibly cut down the detail in another part.

3. *Decide the point of view of the story-teller*

Are you going to tell the story in the third person—the way the extracts given on p. 53 and this page are told? Or will you imagine yourself as one as those there at the time and tell it in the first person? If you decide on this second method, are you going to be

95

the main character—Zacchaeus, for example—or one of the minor characters—someone in the crowd who had suffered through Zacchaeus' greed?

How to tell the story

Good story telling will be marked by:

1. *A good beginning*.
   The first sentence needs to grip the attention and awaken interest. Let it be about a person and some action, or be direct speech, not straight description of a scene.

2. Develop the story swiftly. Do not let it drag. Build up to a climax.

3. Remember *why* you are telling the story, making sure that the point of the story is clear but without adding it on at the end.

4. Use plenty of direct speech—conversation or sometimes 'thinking aloud'. Make sure this is in contemporary language.

5. Use vivid words that spur on the imagination—'he scurried' or 'he dawdled' paints a much clearer picture than 'he went'. Avoid vague, colourless words. Do not clutter the story with too many adjectives, however: you want to make the story live, not to slow it down.

6. Use all of yourself in telling the story. Practise on your own at home or—better still—in front of an honest friend or a tape-recorder. Your facial expression can be a valuable visual aid. So can a few gestures—but do not overdo this! In using your voice, vary the speed and the volume. Hushed tones and occasional pauses can build up suspense. Increasing speed can add excitement.

7. Build up to a dramatic climax, to be followed by the briefest possible ending—one or two sentences which need specially careful preparation. Then stop!

What does this story teach?

Here is the beginning of a re-telling of the story of Peter's release from prison (Acts 12. 1–17). As you read it, ask what teaching is being given through it. If possible, read it aloud so that you can practise the suggestions given in 6 above.

'Clank! Clank! The two chains, with which Peter was bound, made such a loud noise in the stillness of the night and pulled on his arms as he tried to turn over in his sleep. Peter woke, shivered

96

as he stirred and felt the cold stone of the prison floor striking through his garment . . . and lay thinking for a moment.

'Was this the cell in which his friend James had waited just a few days earlier . . . waited for Herod to decide what should be done with him? And now James was dead . . . he was with the Lord. Perhaps the same two soldiers had stood guard over him the night before Herod had had him killed?

'They'd all prayed for James, back in the houses here and there in the city where the Christians met together in groups to worship and share what God was teaching them. There were over five thousand of them now—and a few weeks earlier there had only been a hundred and twenty.

'Peter smiled. Not even Herod could stop what *God* was doing! Peter could imagine what his friends were doing right now— praying for him, just as they had all prayed for James. But James was killed all the same . . . Peter smiled again. God knew best—He knew what He was doing. And He would do what was right for Peter, too. Tomorrow he might be set free . . . or he might be killed and then he would be with the Lord Jesus again. Peter was not afraid. He prayed that God would keep his mind at peace and then he fell asleep once more.

'Suddenly he woke up again. The cell was full of a strange light, and someone—not a soldier—straightened up. He had shaken Peter awake and now he spoke: "Get up quickly." Peter, feeling as though he must be dreaming, stood up . . . and the chains fell off his hands! "Get dressed and put on your sandals," said the man. The soldiers had not moved. Why didn't they stop the man? He was not one of them. It must be a dream.

"Right—wrap your cloak round yourself and follow me."

'They passed the first set of sentries, and then the second. It was almost as though the soldiers did not even *see* them. Before them now was the iron gate leading out into the street. As they drew near, the gate swung open, although no hand had drawn back the bolts and opened it. Down the first street they went—and suddenly the stranger was gone. Peter realized that he *was* awake, not dreaming—and he *was* free! He was free!

'"The Lord has sent an angel," he said, "and rescued me from Herod." And he hurried on through the dark, quiet streets to where he knew his friends would be praying for him.'

97

Evoking a response

If we *really* make our teaching live for the children, it will not just absorb their minds and stimulate their thinking. It will provoke response of some kind. Our teaching may, of course, be rejected, and we should never forget that if our teaching is any good at all, Satan will be actively seeking to counter it with his own lies. He may attempt to persuade one child that 'it's all a load of rubbish— Mum and Dad don't believe any of it.' He may distract another child with thoughts about something quite different, or accuse another of not being good enough for God. However good our teaching may be, it will achieve nothing of itself, but must be prepared and given prayerfully and in the power of the Holy Spirit. Nehemiah's men used tools in rebuilding the walls of Jerusalem, and we need the 'tools of the trade'—the teaching techniques—but they also needed weapons against the enemy (Neh. 4. 17, 18), and so do we. The more effectively we wield the spiritual weapons we have been given, weapons which have 'divine power to destroy strongholds' (2 Cor. 10. 4), the more we shall see children responding as we teach them. We need to learn how to use the authority of the name of Jesus, and to pray in faith, and to open ourselves more and more for the Holy Spirit to teach others through us.

Chapter Ten

USING THEIR EYES

What does a manufacturer do when he wants to sell a new product? He advertises it. How? Usually with both words *and* pictures—in printed advertisements in newspapers and periodicals, on posters, on television, by any means open to him. How much impact would they have if they had words only?

Let's look at the value of using visual aids in our teaching.

WHAT VISUAL AIDS CAN DO

Helping the understanding

It is possible for a child to form such an incorrect mental picture that the teaching ceases to make sense. The visual aid that would help here is the one that gives information—the picture or filmstrip that shows the background to life in Bible times, for example. The child who pictures a house with a pointed roof and a loft between that and the bedrooms will find it difficult to imagine the four men lowering their paralysed friend through a hole in the roof to the Lord Jesus Christ. If they imagine the man in the type of bed used in their own homes they will have even more difficulty! A picture—even a quick sketch—or a model would help the child to understand.

Focusing the attention

The teaching was to be on Joseph, but Miss Green had tried to set up what would look something like a television studio—without the cameras. The children's attention was immediately caught by the notice, 'Studio 1', and by the microphone (a shampoo bottle wrapped in cooking foil and inverted on a piece of stick nailed to a wooden base). A length of flex trailed away to a point behind Miss Green. She had been very careful to make sure it was not *too* close to the children. Gary would certainly have been tempted to 'plug himself in'! With the children's interest aroused Miss Green could begin. The 'microphone' had focused their attention.

Stimulating thought
'Welcome to *The World This Morning*. This week we are taking a look at unsuccessful people—people who have not got on well in life. First of all, let's look at this man.' Miss Green held up a picture she had found in a magazine of someone suffering from severe malnutrition, and began questioning the children. The visual aid this time was intended to stimulate thought and provoke discussion.

Emphasizing reality
Children are often helped to grasp the fact that Biblical history is what really happened in a real place if they see places marked on a map. We must remember, however, that the 7–8 year-old may not have been introduced to the idea of maps, and what is meaningful to you will then be a squiggly pattern of lines to him. Even with older Juniors it helps to—

● Use a simple sketch map rather than a complicated one with scores of different places named.

● Colour the sea and lakes blue so that children are clear as to which side of a line is water and which is land.

● Label any place which appeared on a map shown to them on some other occasion, so that children begin to absorb where places were in relation to one another.

● Give a local comparative distance to explain the scale (e.g., Galilee to Jerusalem and Margate to London—70 miles).

It is not difficult to learn to draw a simple sketch map showing the Sea of Galilee, the River Jordan, and the Dead Sea. The coastline of the eastern side of the Mediterranean Sea for this section is very simple indeed. Learn where to place Nazareth and Jerusalem for a start. Other places can be added as you grow more confident— but the effect of being able to draw such a map quickly in front of the children will give them a good impression of your capabilities.

Another kind of map which interests children and helps to emphasize reality is one built up from a number of sheets of polystyrene. You will need a map which gives contour lines on which to base this. By using such a map, you will be able to show that Jericho and the Dead Sea are below sea level, and that the road between

Jericho and Jerusalem in the Judean hills rises very steeply. Places can be named by pushing flags made from printed sticks and gummed labels into the appropriate place. Print the place-name on the flag— but not in block capitals.

Helping the memory

One of the most helpful kinds of visual aid to use in teaching is the one that builds up a summary of the teaching or that expresses visually the truth that is in the aim for that particular session. These can be entirely in words (as long as the children can read), or entirely in pictures, or in a mixture of the two.

Three simple flash-cards could be used with a lesson on Joseph forgiving his brothers—three pieces of card bearing the words 'Joseph forgave', 'God forgives' and 'We must forgive'. These would help children to remember the truth behind the story, expressed in the aim 'To show that God requires us to be forgiving as He is forgiving.'

A WARNING

A Bible story can be summarized quite easily in a series of simple pictures—but it is not so easy to summarize a *spiritual* truth in pictures alone. We can easily fall into the danger of misleading a child. An example of this is the use of a heart. The Biblical use of the word 'heart' means the centre of one's will and thinking—*not* the seat of the emotions as in present-day popular use in songs, Valentine's Day cards and colloquialisms about a broken heart, *nor* the physical organ pumping the blood around the body which can, in some cases, be removed and a transplant provided. The trouble with drawing a heart and saying that we need to ask Jesus into it, is that the heart-shape suggests either of our modern ideas about the heart and does not immediately imply to a child the centre of one's will and thinking. The image confuses.

The situation is only worsened by showing children a black heart to represent sin. We should take great care *not* to suggest that black is bad and white is good. This is not a Biblical picture (sin is described as being 'like scarlet . . . red like crimson' in Isa. 1. 18), and it may add to racial tensions.

DON'T KILL THE IMAGINATION

If you do use an artist's impression of what a Biblical scene may have looked like—and you might look again at p. 59 under 'Suggestibility and intuition'—it is as well to explain that it *is* only one person's idea. Be sure the picture is really necessary, however, before you use it. We should not use a picture simply so as to have a visual aid if there is nothing else to justify it. The wrong aid can deaden or deny the imagination. An illustration of a Bible story can focus the attention too much on only one *part* of the story. The detail in it can distract a child's attention.

ONLY AN AID

A visiting speaker to a group of Juniors meeting for a school SU group once produced a very absorbing visual aid. It was a model house, so wired to a battery that by touching various switches at the back, different sections lit up. He talked about 'the house of our lives'—but the aid was too enthralling. It became a hindrance and children's minds were not on what he was saying, but on how the lights worked, which part might be lit up next, and whether they themselves could make anything like it.

The first time we use flannelgraph in front of children, it needs to be explained: 'This isn't "magic"; any fluffy material will cling to any other fluffy material,' is sufficient. The children's minds are then free from wondering 'How does it work?' and can concentrate on what is being illustrated.

BE FLEXIBLE

Ideas for visual aids given in a printed outline may need adaptation for use with your particular group. Be prepared to be flexible. Vocabulary may need to be simplified for some children. Materials suggested may not be available, and ideas may need to be put into a different form. It helps, of course, to keep a stock of materials from which visual aids can be made.

MAKING VISUAL AIDS
Materials

1. Keep a store of useful items—boxes, scraps of material, pipe-cleaners, cardboard rolls, cheap lining paper, ends of newsprint rolls (sometimes obtainable very cheaply from the local newspaper printer), off-cuts of paper and card (try a local printer), useful pictures from magazines, scraps of patterned and brown wrapping paper, coloured cellophane, string, egg-boxes, etc. Sugar-paper is a

thicker but still cheap paper, good for mounting pictures on or for children to paint on. Try a shop selling artist's materials. Odd rolls of wallpaper are cheap and very useful. Keep, too, a packet of gummed labels and some coloured gummed paper.

2. Keep together the small items you are likely to use frequently—felt-tipped pens, pencils, a rubber, a ruler, scissors, adhesive tape, paste, glue, paint, brushes, inks, drawing pins, brass-headed paper fasteners, pins, a stapler, and so on.

3. A yard-stick (from a wallpaper shop) will be found very useful indeed.

4. Coloured blotting-paper can be used for flannelgraph pieces (roughen the back with a piece of sandpaper; write on it with a spirit-based felt-tipped pen), and is much cheaper than felt, which might perhaps be kept for making flannelgraph that is to be used many times. Pictures, mounted on thin card, can also have a tiny square of *Teazlegraph* (or *Velcro*—obtainable from the haberdashery department of a local store) stuck on the back. (Use the *Velcro* strip with the tiny nylon hooks and discard the other piece.) This will cling very firmly to a piece of brushed nylon. Although quite expensive, it makes it possible to use flannelgraph even in a breeze in the open air—and the tiny pieces of *Teazlegraph* or *Velcro* can be pulled off the pictures and used again.

5. A variation on flannelgraph is the use of a thin sheet of steel and pictures with tiny pieces of magnetic strip stuck on the back.

Simple picture-making

Children do *not* expect you to be a Rembrandt! Simple pictures you have produced yourself also have two big advantages over the Bible picture bought from a shop:

● they leave plenty of scope for the children's imagination;

● they encourage the children when it comes to *their* turn to draw something.

We may produce pin-men or figures with more body based on thin, elongated triangles. The latter are more effective if coloured solidly—and if the head does not *quite* touch the body and *very* small gaps are left between the triangles.

Alternatively, we can use simple shapes to build up figures as below:

Crowds are very simple to draw if you go back to your scribbling days—

If you want to make the crowd look even bigger with no extra work, draw it so that it is right on one edge of the paper—

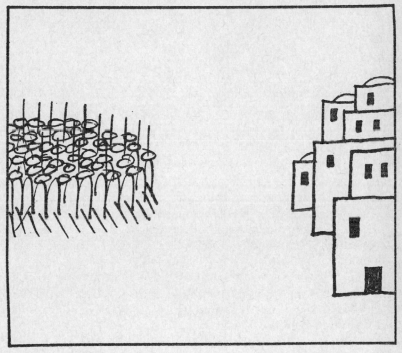

The same thing can be done to draw a city, as is shown on the right of the same picture.

If the crowd is an army, add strokes for spears and others, all at the same angle, to represent legs stepping forward. These legs will show in which direction the army is marching and will give the impression of movement.

Lettering

Road signs giving names of places along a particular route are not written in block capitals. This is because block capitals are not easy to read quickly. For the child who is still a poor reader, they may even prove impossible, as they completely alter the 'shape' of a word and prevent him recognizing it by its appearance. Block capitals should therefore be avoided. So should fancy styles with loops and curls. The simplest is best for children, and this means the simple script lettering which one first learns to write.

Aa Bb Cc Dd Ee Ff Gg Hh Ii
Jj Kk Ll Mm Nn Oo Pp Qq
Rr Ss Tt Uu Vv Ww Xx Yy Zz

Layout and presentation

A picture often looks better if mounted on a piece of paper of a different colour, but the colour should be fairly subdued or it will distract the attention from the picture. Leave a margin of about an inch to the top and sides of the picture, but a wider margin below ($1\frac{1}{2}$" or 2"). If mounting several pictures on one sheet, space them out so that they do not look too crowded.

Some colours show up much better than others. Black or blue lettering on white paper is very clear, red is not quite as distinct, and green will not be legible except to those very close to the sheet of paper. Yellow is even less clear on white. Blue is not as distinct on a green background as black would be.

Make sure that any visual aid is the right size for your group and neither too large nor too small. Lettering will need to be 2" or even 3" high if a large group needs to be able to read it. Do not use the thin-tipped variety of felt pen on any visual aid which needs to be visible over more than a few feet. Experiment with lettering and see what you can read from a distance *before* you use the aid with children. You will find, for example that bold, thick, rounded letters are more legible than bigger letters that are elongated and squashed together—e.g.,

this *is clearer than* †h¡ʃ

Pictures and maps that are too small can be scaled up. Over the original, lightly pencil in lines marking off squares. On your large piece of paper, draw the *same* number of squares. Now copy what is in a square on the small illustration into the equivalent but much larger square on the big sheet, thus:

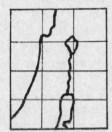
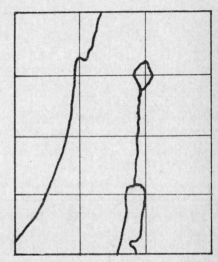

Display boards

Blackboards can be made easily and cheaply from pieces of hardboard, painted with 'blackboard paint'—a special matt paint produced for this purpose. The rough side of hardboard can be used as it is for a flannelgraph background, or it can be covered with any fluffy material.

Chalkboards do not *have* to be black, of course: a dark green is a good colour—especially if yellow chalk is used. Use a matt paint, not a gloss finish.

Insulating board is useful for displaying pictures, as drawing pins can be pushed into it very easily.

A clothes airer and a bulldog clip can be utilised, too, as a display stand.

AIDS MADE BY CHILDREN

Mention has already been made of activities at the beginning of a programme when children may be given friezes, models, books, etc., to make—and these, of course, are visual aids, too.

Here it is important not to provide activity simply for the sake of giving children an opportunity to make something. The thing which is finally produced must be worthwhile in itself *to the child*, however crude it might appear to adult eyes, and it must teach a truth, or stimulate imagination, or remind children of a previous lesson.

STORING VISUAL AIDS

'This was our coal cellar until we switched to gas heating,' said the proud owner as she flung open the door. There in front of her visitor was shelf upon shelf of visual materials.

Few of us, however, have such an opportunity to accumulate and store all the equipment needed for the Junior Department of a Sunday School. The notes which follow may give ideas to those who have less space but who still want to keep their own equipment tidy and unobtrusive.

A set of wall pockets—although intended for the storage of shoes, a hanging set of pockets, made from strong, transparent plastic, is a useful way of keeping together the smaller items of equipment. Screw a cup-hook into the inside of a cupboard door, and hang these wall-pockets there. You will know where everything is, and it will be out of the way until required.

Cardboard 'wallets'—made from thin card, obtainable from good stationers for approximately 5p (foolscap size), are useful for holding pictures cut from magazines.

A large box on castors—designed to fit beneath a single bed. This can be made quite cheaply as good quality wood is not necessary. The lid is a sheet of hardboard with lengths of 1" timber fastened to it so that they just fit inside the top rim of the box. Drawer handles and castors make it easy to pull out the box when required. It will hold a large quantity of rolls of paper, folders of pictures cut from magazines, *Adventurers*, maps and charts which you may require again, etc.

Visual aids no longer required? You may well find that children take great pleasure in being given a visual aid to take home—but make sure you are not going to want to display it at a parents' evening or use it again in a following 'lesson'.

USING VISUAL AIDS
Practise beforehand
Whatever aid you are going to use, practise with it beforehand. Children will grow bored and restless while you search for the right piece of flannelgraph, or try to push something into slots that are too small, or realize that you ought to have changed the plug on the projector.

Make sure all the children can see
This means placing the aid at the right height. If it is too low, one child's view will be blocked by the head of another.

Chapter Eleven

HANDS TOGETHER AND EYES CLOSED?

Ten-year-old Alison had just started Sunday School. That very day she was able to suggest something that might be prayed about. The leader asked, 'Would you like to say it yourself for us, Alison—just a sentence, and we'll say "Amen" at the end?'

'Oh, I couldn't possibly,' replied Alison. 'I mean I don't know the right words to use—all the Thee's and Thou's that the Vicar uses. I couldn't do that.'

One of the other children spoke up. 'You don't have to do that, Alison. We can talk to God in ordinary words—like when we talk to anyone else.'

So Alison did—but what she had previously learnt indirectly about prayer had discouraged her from praying. How can we lead children in prayer so that we teach *them* to pray, too?

CHILDREN AND PRAYER

Once again, the children must be participants—not just those over whose heads a whole stream of words is poured. Prayer-time can too easily become play-time if the prayer is in adult language, dealing with what an adult thinks should be mentioned in prayer, and going on . . . and on . . . and on.

One group of bored children once built a whole tower from kneelers in front of their praying leader—whose eyes were devoutly closed. In another group, a child at the front solemnly beat time to the drone of his leader's voice, while the other children watched and giggled. The leader—the only one with his eyes closed—prayed on . . *but the children were not praying*.

Leading children in prayer means just that . . . not praying one's own private prayer in their company. How are we to do it?

LEADING IN PRAYER
Pray about things children understand.

Remember children's experience of life. Confession of sin in adult terms will not do, for example. Here is a prayer about sin (but not using that word) that mirrors children's experience:

'Lord Jesus, please stop us from thinking that it's funny or clever to be naughty, that it doesn't really matter if we do *little* things that are wrong. Keep us from feeling that it's all right to do wrong if others are doing it. Please help us not to pretend that we are good. For Your sake. Amen'*

Pray in their language
'O Lord our God, it is a good thing to give praise to You, for You are the Lord most high. Your works are great, and Your thoughts are very clever. You are the same since before the world began. We thank You that You do not change. Amen.'

Notice that 'their language' also involves using the language of today e.g., 'You' rather than 'Thou'. 'Your thoughts are very clever' may not be in the beautiful language of hundreds of years ago, nor in the language of Scripture, nor in theological language—but children can understand it and mean it for themselves. Their 'Amen' can then *mean* something—if they have also been taught what 'Amen' itself means!

Be imaginative
The more we try to imagine what children's everyday life is like, the better equipped we shall be to lead them in prayers that are relevant to them. Take this as an example of a prayer relating to helping, firmly based on what helping at school means to a child:

'Father God, please make us into helpers at school, offering to stay in, even on sunny days, to wash the paint brushes, wiping up things that get spilt on the floor and washing the cloth out afterwards, tying up the skipping rope before putting it away, staying behind to look for the lost ball, carrying things for our teachers, and putting up the chairs on the empty desks at the end of the day. Because we want to please the Lord Jesus, we ask it. Amen.'

Ask for children's suggestions
Give them some help, however! 'What shall we pray about today?'

---

*Prayers in this chapter are taken from *Let's talk to God*, by Zinnia Bryan, published by Scripture Union.

is likely to lead to the same vague list of generalizations every time the question is asked. Make the question more specific, e.g., 'We are going to have a "Thank You" prayer now. Think of something you have seen or done today that makes you want to say "Thank You"' or 'We are going to pray for people who have to work today. Who are these people? What do you think we should ask for them?'

Be brief
A child's attention span is short. Although one child might be able to continue in real, heartfelt prayer for some time, we are likely to be leading a *group* of varied spiritual experience—and none! We must be brief. Two minutes is long enough. Another two-minute time of prayer can follow at another point in the programme.

RESPONSIVE PRAYERS
A short sentence of response, such as 'We thank You' or 'We are sorry, Lord' can be said after phrases spoken by the leader. This is usually better than children repeating a whole prayer, phrase by phrase, after the leader, as they tend to lose the meaning of a sentence that is split up into several phrases. The line of response must also be kept short, of course, or children will not remember what they are supposed to say.

WHAT ABOUT SET PRAYERS?
A prayer written by someone else, not even in the group, can be as helpful as one made up at the time it is spoken. The prayer should be one that children *can* understand, however, even if a few words or phrases need explaining first. The Lord's Prayer needs to be explained if children are to say it with understanding rather than as something they can do automatically while their minds are on something else. It may sometimes be helpful to have a prayer written out and read by the children.

CHILDREN CAN WRITE PRAYERS
This is often suggested as part of a 'lesson' in *Teaching Juniors*. It helps a child to think of what he has learnt and apply it to himself personally. Children can write prayers for special occasions, too, such as a Family Carol Service or a Harvest Service. Prayers that are of general use—not the very personal ones—can be kept in a

special book, with a decorative cover made by one or more of the children. These prayers can then be used as and when appropriate.

CHILDREN CAN LEAD IN PRAYER
Boys and girls who suggest prayer topics can be asked if they would like to say it themselves in a one- or two-sentence prayer. In this way they learn to pray aloud in their own words in front of other people at an age when they are not as self-conscious as they will be as teenagers or adults. It is not unknown for there to be more volunteers than there is time for, once this idea becomes established. There will often be a marked increase in attention when it is children who are leading in prayer.

It is important, however, not to have *all* prayer led in this way, as children's prayers can become stereotyped. (So can those of adults . . . and it is a good thing if *different* members of the teaching team lead in prayer and it is not always one person who does it.)

DIFFERENT KINDS OF PRAYER
'Sorry', 'Thank You', and 'Please' are simple, straightforward ways of describing prayers of confession, thanksgiving, petition and intercession. Children are very familiar with the words 'sorry', 'thank you' and 'please', and to apply these to prayer enables us to go from the familiar to the unfamiliar—an important principle in teaching.

Praise must not be neglected, however. It *can* be seen as falling within the category of 'Thank You' prayers, as we praise God *and* thank Him for what He is. An example of such a prayer was given on p. 111.

Some hymns and choruses are prayers set to music and this should be pointed out to children.

PRAYER CHARTS
Children can collect pictures from magazines which show suitable subjects for prayer. These could be made to slit into a chart with three 'picture-frames', labelled 'Sorry', 'Thank You' and 'Please'. A child can sometimes be chosen to decide which pictures should be displayed, and either a leader or volunteers from the children can describe the picture and ask what ideas it gives for prayer. Prayers can then be said silently or by the person who asked for the suggestions.

PRAYER IS A RESPONSE

It can be our response to something discussed, to something looked at, or to something learnt. If it is a response to something looked at it could accompany a series of transparencies showing beautiful sights, each accompanied by a one-sentence 'Thank You' prayer. In this case, of course, the children will keep their eyes open, for what they are looking at will not be a distraction but the subject of their prayer.

A few moments of silence are often well used in a prayer that is a response to something learnt. Juniors really can use a brief silence—if their own feelings have been aroused about the subject of the prayer-time.

THINK ABOUT CHILDREN'S PHYSICAL POSITION

Avoid any position that will be too uncomfortable or that will take children out of your sight (such as kneeling behind high pews). If children are standing with their eyes closed, they may begin to sway and have to open their eyes to regain their balance. Sitting is usually the most reverent and helpful position for a group of Juniors. 'Heads bowed' may suggest humility to us, but it may not convey this idea at all to children and is not necessarily the best habit to teach. Some adults find it more helpful to raise the head as though looking up to God in order to receive—and we should not impose a rigid pattern upon a child so that he feels prayer *must* be with 'hands together and eyes closed.' 'Hands together' certainly stops them fiddling with other things—but it is not the *only* attitude hands may take in prayer. Again, some adults in their own prayer-time like to hold their hands cupped as they pray, or raise them in worship, and we should not so teach children that, meeting with these different ways of worship in later life, in their own or in other countries, they feel shocked because the outward attitudes are different. These are mere externals, part perhaps of our custom, but not on a level with the truth about God that we are teaching. We do not need to regiment children into a pattern that may be a hindrance to them later on.

BE REAL

Of course, discipline is going to concern us. Yet we must not so glare at every child who opens his eyes and feel that we never dare close our own that *we* are merely saying a string of words without really praying from the heart. Children are quick to sense what does not really mean much to us, and worship is going to be caught rather than taught anyway. It we really praise God as we lead the children's praise, they are likely to 'catch' something of what we feel and sense that we do indeed know that God is there, and that He is great and wonderful, and that we rejoice in belonging to Him.

Chapter Twelve

WHAT ABOUT MUSIC?

No, not just singing, but listening and playing and moving to music, too. Deciding that's not for your group? Then let's begin with singing.

How many mistakes can you discover here? Mr. Bloggs is describing his Sunday School.

'Every week we start with a quarter of an hour's chorus singing. This gives the children a chance to let off steam. I encourage them to try to "raise the roof" and sometimes have the boys competing against the girls, so we get some good, lusty singing. They enjoy it. Sometimes we have action choruses like "Running over, running over" or "We are climbing Jacob's ladder." The children also like "Give me oil in my lamp"—it's got a good tune. I let the children choose the first few every week. Then later on we have two or three hymns—the sort they're likely to meet with in church, like "I will sing the wondrous story" and "The King of love my Shepherd is." '

HOW MUCH SINGING?

A quarter of an hour at the beginning and then two or three more hymns is likely to be too much, for the 9–11 year old boys especially. The older Junior boy's least-liked school subject is often singing, and if we find the boys stop coming towards the top of the age-group, too much singing could be a part of the reason. It is better to err on the side of having too little and leaving the children wanting more, than to have too much and drive them away. Two or three hymns, songs or choruses—not two or three of each—is for most Junior groups, a reasonable amount in an hour's programme.

WHY SING AT ALL?

'To give children a chance to let off steam' is not a good enough reason. It that's all it means to the children, they might as well sing secular songs. (That could even be better than singing Christian songs without giving a thought to the words—merely to see how much noise can be made.)

The competition between boys and girls to see who can sing the more loudly is pointless, too, and encourages shouting instead of singing. Is such competition really a right thing, anyway? Look back to p. 30.

WHAT SHALL WE SING?

Look at some of the words being sung by Mr. Bloggs' group. In your mind put a cross beside any line that is not in every child's experience. Put a further cross if figurative or 'picture' language is being used, which might be taken the wrong way, or if the language is too difficult for a Junior:

Running over, running over, my cup's filled and running over . . .
Since the Lord saved me, I'm as happy as can be . . .
We are climbing Jacob's ladder, soldiers of the cross . . .
Give me oil in my lamp, keep me burning . . .
I will sing the wondrous story . . . I was lost but Jesus found me . . .
Faint was I from many a fall . . .
Days of darkness still come o'er me, sorrow's paths I often tread . . .
Where the verdant pastures grow, with food celestial feedeth . . .
Thy unction grace bestoweth, and O what transport of delight from Thy pure chalice floweth . . .

Of course, there are other lines in those hymns and choruses that *are* simple and straightforward, and that do not speak subjectively of an experience a child has not had, but they are in the minority. Each item would take too much explaining, and is better not sung by our matter-of-fact Juniors.

The following questions give a guide to deciding what is and what is not suitable. Try asking them of some of the items you sing with the children.

1. Is it meaningful? Do the boys and girls themselves know the experiences being expressed? (This question would cut out the items that are about specifically *Christian* experience like 'My cup's filled and running over' or that express adult feelings like 'Sorrow's paths I often tread.')

117

2. Are the experiences it mentions expressed in language children can understand? (Do not discard a whole hymn for the sake of one word, however: it could be explained. It is a different matter when a lot of difficult words are used, as in 'The King of Love', where a simpler hymn also based on Psalm 23 could be sung instead. If one verse is difficult, but could be omitted, leave out that one verse.)

3. Is it the right language for the age-group—Juniors—or is it too 'babyish'? (Avoid 'little children' and 'little hands'. Do not sing at all an item which Juniors will think completely 'beneath' them, like 'I have hands that can clap, clap, clap.')

4. Do the words have value in themselves as an expression of Biblical truth? (How does 'I am H-A-P-P-Y' stand up against this one?)

5. Does the mood of the music (joyous, thoughtful, etc.) fit the words? Tunes do not all have to be solemn, but words and tune should both set the same 'mood' or atmosphere. The tune should be worthy of the spiritual content of the words that go with it and help a child to develop an appreciation for what is really good, not just trivial.

6. Is the tune easy enough for a child to be able to remember it and sing it on his own at home if he wanted to?

7. Is the tune the only reason for singing a particular item? If so, think again!

HOW TO TEACH A NEW HYMN

How do children get to know popular songs? Usually it is by hearing them over and over again. No one stands up and says 'Now repeat these words after me . . . Listen to the tune . . . sing the first line . . .'

The easiest way in fact for a child to learn a new hymn or chorus is by hearing it sung. If it is very simple, he may well be able to join in the second time. He may have already heard the new tune without thinking much about it, as it could have been played before the session began and while children were still arriving.

If one of the leaders can bring himself—or herself—to sing the words to the children without collapsing in a red-faced, self-conscious heap, it really *will* help the children. . . and they will not be as critical of our voices as we may expect them to be if we do not pretend to be what we are not. Children do understand if a leader says, 'I'm no good at singing—I haven't much of a voice—but I'll have a go so that you can hear more or less what it's like.' If we're not afraid to make mistakes, children will not be afraid either.

The accompaniment to a new hymn or chorus should emphasize the melody line rather than the other notes that provide the harmonic backing.

ACCOMPANIMENT FOR SINGING

No piano?

If you do have a piano, try to position it so that the treble end (the high notes) is nearer to the children than the bass notes. This means that they will hear the line of melody more clearly.

If you have no pianist or no piano, can you make use of a tape recorder and get a friend or church member who plays the piano to record accompaniments for you? Work out how many verses you need for each item and tell your pianist beforehand. Also ask for the first line or, if more suitable in some items, the first two lines to be played as an introduction. Children do not then need the note to be given. The giving of a note before every verse is not, in fact, helpful anyway as it breaks the rhythm. Nor is it necessary once an introductory verse has been played or a preceding verse sung.

With a tape-recorded accompaniment, a regular rhythm is very important, and it is helpful to have a slightly more pronounced beat than would be used with live accompaniment.

On the box in which you keep the tape, list the items on it in their correct order, and the number of verses which each has.

What about other instruments?

A guitar accompaniment may be preferable with some items. Make use of any one who can play this—or any other instrument if it can be used in accompaniment.

Sing to God (published by Scripture Union with music and words editions) which contains a selection of hymns, choruses and Christian songs, both traditional and modern, chosen for Juniors in accordance with the questions given on p. 117, has simple guitar as well as piano accompaniments. The two are not always meant to be played together, however, as simple guitar chords have been given, rather than more difficult ones used in the piano accompaniment.

Children can make percussion instruments, and provide their

119

own simple 'rhythm group' (a name which will appeal more than 'percussion band' to Juniors). Here are some instruments that can be made simply and cheaply:

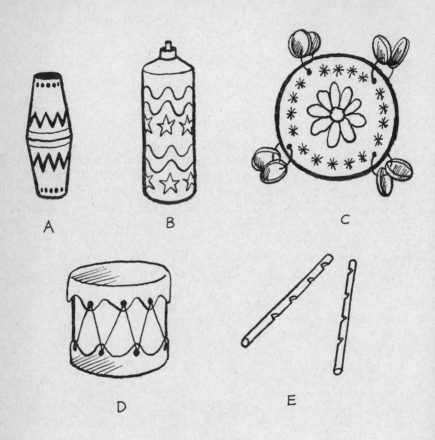

A.   B.   C

D   E

A. *Two plastic cartons and a handful of dried peas or rice.*

1. Remove words from cartons with sandpaper or wire-wool soap pad.
2. Decorate with felt-tipped pens but not the watercolour variety.
3. Fill one carton one-third full with dried peas or rice.
4. Bind the two cartons together with decorator's masking tape.
5. Shake to play.

B. *Washing-up liquid container and dried peas or rice.*
1. Remove words on container as above.
2. Decorate as above.
3. Unscrew stopper, insert dried peas or rice, and replace stopper.
4. Shake to play.

C. *Cardboard plate and milk-bottle tops.*
1. Decorate plate (e.g., with felt-tipped pens).
2. Punch four holes around rim of plate.
3. Punch a hole in eight milk-bottle tops.
4. Loosely tie two milk-bottle tops with coloured wool through each hole in the plate.
5. Play as you would a tambourine—shake or tap.

D. *Two short lengths of dowelling.*
1. Cut dowelling into short lengths, approx. 9″ long.
2. File notches across each rod. (The notches do not need to go right round each rod.)
3. Decorate the rods with felt-tipped pens.
4. Play by either rubbing up and down or by tapping one on the other.

E. *Caterer's size jam tins* (7 *lbs.*) *and discarded car inner tube.*
(Ask children to approach school meals' cooks for tins—select *one* child per school!—and car-owner relatives for inner tubes.)
1. Remove bottom of tin and paint with household gloss paint.
2. Cut two circles of rubber at least 3″ bigger in diameter than the tin.
3. Pierce holes 1″ from edge of rubber circle and 2″ apart.
4. Lace together the two rubber circles at top and bottom of tin, using a length of strong string (see diagram).
5. Hold between knees and play with fingers, African-drum style.

Children who play the recorder can be encouraged to form a group and given simple tunes to practise and then play in accompaniment to singing. (Find out from the children which notes they can and cannot play; they may be very much beginners! Do not choose any tune with notes below middle C.)

In some items—e.g., 'Come and praise the Lord our King'—clapping can provide a very suitable accompaniment.

MUSIC FOR LISTENING
Do you remember how music was being played softly as children arrived for Mr. Maxwell's Sunday group (p. 73)? This was planned

to set the right atmosphere. Tapes and records of children's choirs singing hymns and choruses and of Christian folk groups can be used—but so can instrumental music. This may be 'serious' music, or folk music, or hymn-tunes. To select suitable music, ask yourself as you listen how it would make you feel if you were a child. A cathedral choir item may not be suitable—but nor may a very loud, Christian beat group! Think of the atmosphere you want and the children you have.

Sometimes a record of a group or solo voice singing an item which you want to teach to the children can be played at the beginning of the session and then again when you want the children to learn it. The children could then sing with the record.

Occasionally, a very short item can be played as part of the programme for children to listen to it and think about what they have been learning—e.g., the Hallelujah chorus from Handel's *Messiah*, after teaching about Christ's ascension, can become a vehicle for worship as one listens if one thinks about Christ, reigning now in Heaven and returning one day to reign over all men.

CHILDREN AS SONG WRITERS

It is not beyond Juniors to write their own very simple items. They will find it easiest to begin by taking an easy tune where only one line needs to be written to have a whole verse—e.g., Kumbaya. Then take a simple four-line tune and let children make up a verse—not necessarily with rhyme—to fit it, e.g., an additional verse of their own to 'Thank You for every new good morning'. New words can then be written to well-known hymn tunes such as 'Onward Christian soldiers', or to pop tunes.

MUSIC FOR MOVEMENT

With some groups this might be a real possibility for use in an 'anniversary' programme, for example. The important things are:
1. A leader who has some idea what 'movement to music' means. (Listen, if you can, to a few of the schools radio broadcasts in this field.)
2. A leader who can think of how movements of different kinds could accompany the telling of a Bible story or a group of children who could do this. If the children do a lot of this kind of activity in school, they may well be able to produce the ideas.

3. A leader with enough knowledge of music to be able to find records, tapes, or piano music to give the right musical 'background'.
4. Sufficient space.
5. Children who are accustomed to such activity at school and who will enjoy taking part.
6. Enthusiasm on the part of the leader—and preferably a willingness to demonstrate any idea. The leader who is not too self-conscious will help the children to be natural.

'I'M NOT MUSICAL!'

God has not chosen to make us all alike, and we do not all have the same gifts. Why not let the musical aspect of the programme be in the hands of the most musical member of the teaching team? Another possibility is to look among the church members for someone who is not prepared to teach, but who would give you musical advice and help, perhaps play the piano, or compile a list of suitable music for listening?

Don't let's forget the children either. They can help tremendously by giving us lists of what they sing at school and of which hymns and choruses they particularly like. There may be one or two who can write choruses—words and even tunes—at home.

'A JOYFUL NOISE'?

If we want a programme in which children can participate fully, we must give them both opportunities to take part and encouragement, and be prepared to be enthusiastic ourselves. We do not have to be beautiful singers ourselves to do this: God is delighted if our praise of Him is joyous and real whatever our natural voices may be like.

> *Clap your hands, all peoples!*
> *Shout to God with loud songs of joy!* . . .
> *God has gone up with a shout,*
> *the Lord with the sound of a trumpet.*
> *Sing praises to God, sing praises!*
> *Sing praises to our King, sing praises!*
> Psa. 47. 1, 5, 6.

Let us pray for—and work towards—the same enjoyment and exultation in praise as the Psalmist expresses in these words. As boys and girls grow in their knowledge of the Lord Jesus Christ through our teaching, and respond to Him in faith and loving obedience through the work of the Holy Spirit, we and they together shall rejoice in the Lord. Then we shall know indeed that our work of leading and teaching the children is not a duty to be carried out merely because we must—but a delight. 'Sing praises to God, sing praises!'

There is a correspondence course based on this book and also a 'Do-it-yourself' training programme (with suggestions for discussion, practical work and the showing of sound-strips). For details, write to the Sunday School Department, Scripture Union, 5 Wigmore Street, London W1H 0AD.

another paperback
published by Scripture Union

FIVE PLUS

by Pamela Dowman

Five Plus is the Primary Department parallel to the book you have just read.

What do we do with the five to sevens and *how*? Do we just let them sing and draw? Or cram in as much Bible doctrine as we can?

Five Plus answers both the *what* and the *how*. It sets out clear Biblical aims for Sunday School primary departments and similar activities. And it is also full of realistic advice and help on understanding this age group, on telling Bible stories, on all kinds of visual aids, on programmes and participation, and the use of music – and on leading children to a personal relationship with Jesus Christ.

Pamela Dowman is Editor of the Scripture Union magazine *Teaching Primaries;* she has been a day school teacher, and is widely known as a speaker at training courses for Sunday School teachers.

a Scripture Union
music publication

SING TO GOD

edited by Margaret Old and Elspeth Stephenson

170 Christian songs especially designed for the 8 to 12 age group. An all-in book containing both hymns and choruses, with a careful balance of old favourites and items related to the world and experience of today's children, together with a good choice of Christian songs. The music is scored for piano, with simple guitar chords. The music edition is a firmly-bound, laminated hard-back in landscape format with an attractive coloured cover design. The words edition, including prayers for group use, is bound in linline.